Read;
Cook;
et
Enjoy!
Berkeley Annex

ADVENTURES in Bubby Irma's Kitchen

A Collection of Treasured Recipes

ADVENTURES in Bubby Irma's Kitchen

A Collection of Treasured Recipes

Irma Charles

TARGUM / FELDHEIM

First published 1992

Copyright © 1992 by Irma Charles
ISBN 0-944070-95-7

Phototypeset at Targum Press

Published by:
Targum Press Inc.
22700 W. Eleven Mile Rd.
Southfield, Mich. 48034

Distributed by:
Feldheim Publishers
200 Airport Executive Park
Spring Valley, N.Y. 10977

Distributed in Israel by:
Nof Books Ltd.
POB 43170
Jerusalem 91430

Printed in Israel

CONTENTS

Acknowledgments

I am thankful to Hashem who has allowed me, even after all these years, to enter into His world and given me the opportunity to learn about Torah and mitzvos.

A special note of thanks to all of my adopted Yeshiva boys, who were always eager to taste the foods, and to their wives who became my good friends. These are treasured relationships.

To all the girls of Eyaht: Aish HaTorah College of Jewish Studies for Women — for their help in keeping my kitchen clean while I cook for Shabbos.

There were and still are so many wonderful young people who pass through our house that it would take another book to talk about each one.

To Linda Sterling: who insisted that I take this book out of the computer and get it to the publishers. I am forever grateful to her.

To my lifelong friend Bernice Landsburg and her family for their support and love.

To Barnea Selavan and David Wilner who kept after me to get this book written.

I have a special connection to many of the families of the Yeshiva students: the Barons, the Coopersmiths, the Gilmans, the Pamenskys, the Sauers, the Shores, the Spiros, and the Sterlings. I am forever grateful to them for raising these beautiful children who make my house a home.

Dedication

This book is dedicated first to my husband, Natie, the cowboy who spurred me on — who nagged and teased me all through the writing of this book. Without him there would be no book.

Next, to my children: Vicki, Debi, and Moshe, who encouraged me all along the road. And to Erika, my first granddaughter, who brought joy into the house when she decided to live in Israel. She is a fabulous gourmet cook on her own. Sharing the kitchen with Erika is a cook's dream. She is always ready to experiment with me.

And to Timna, Andreia, Aaron Michael, Shira, and Elyse: the perfect grandchildren. If you don't believe me, ask Natie.

To my readers:

Read my stories, enjoy cooking my recipes, and meet my family and friends. I will be happy to answer any questions and look forward to meeting you in Israel.

Bubby Irma
4 Hatamid
Old City, Jerusalem, Israel

Elul 5753
September 1992

From the Desk of
Rabbi Noach Weinberg

One of the best Jerusalem experiences you can have is to enjoy a meal with Bubby Irma and Zadie Natie. Failing that, the next best thing you can do is to read and use Bubby Irma's cookbook.

In their home across from the Temple Mount, the Charleses have loved and cared for many of our students, dispensing wisdom and a bowl of chicken soup for anyone in need of some T.L.C. (Tender Loving Care). Their warmth and hospitality is of almost legendary status in the eyes of their family, friends, and many hundreds of guests.

Irma and Natie and this wonderful book give tremendous insight into what Judaism is really about. Enjoy!!

Sincerely,
Rabbi Noach Weinberg
Rosh HaYeshiva, Aish Hatorah Yeshiva

From the Desk of
Rabbi Yitzchak Berkovits

There are no sure-fire recipes when it comes to Jewish education. It's almost as if we stand by and observe as young men and women, initially with little appreciation of Jewish values, become committed, proud Jews, build beautiful families, and go on to dedicate their lives to serving Klal Yisrael.

There are, however, some ingredients that help facilitate these miracles — stimulating educational programs, dedicated educators, and most basic of all — the wisdom of a Jewish grandmother.

Bubby Irma Charles is for so many of our students the sympathetic ear, the caring heart, the source of encouragement, and, with piercing insight, the graceful scolding finger.

This book takes the reader right into the Charleses' "kitchen beis midrash" with its food, warmth, and wisdom.

May Hashem bless the Charleses with the strength and means to keep their doors open for many many years to come.

Yitzchak Berkovits
Aish HaTorah Yeshiva
Jerusalem

16 Sivan 5752

From the Desk of
Rav Matis Weinberg

We sometimes forget the truly fundamental role that food plays in Judaism. Food to the Jew is more than a grand accompaniment to holidays and Shabbat; more than a warm setting for life's special moments. Food is the theme of the relationship between humanity and God as enshrined in the covenant with Noah; a central motif of the mitzvot relating to the sanctity of the Jewish people; and the mitzvah around which Jewish identity coalesced in Egypt and is renewed every year at the Pesach seder. Because food, after all, is nothing less than the most primal focal point of our relationship to the world outside ourselves.

Bubby Irma and Uncle Natie Charles don't even need to think about all that. Food has been a natural part of their inborn genius for relationship, and they have certainly made the most of it; hospitality, philosophy, down-to-earth advice, kiruv, and chessed are all wrapped up together in every dish they serve.

Here's an opportunity to taste some of the spice and share some of the spirit of their marvelous Yerushalayim kitchen overlooking the Kotel HaMaaravi. Savor it well!

Matis Weinberg

ADVENTURES IN BUBBY IRMA'S KITCHEN

For six years I have been nagged, teased, and embarrassed about this cookbook. What ever made me think it would be easy? What ever made me think that I could be clever enough to actually put all my recipes into writing?

When we read a cookbook we assume that the author knows a lot about the nutritional values of food. Let me assure you, I do not. One may also assume that the author is a gourmet cook. Again, let me dispel that theory. Then, you might ask, "Why is Bubby Irma writing this book?" The answer is that I have been cooking for forty-five years and I love it. If I am depressed, I go into the kitchen and cook. If I am happy, I cook up a storm. Cooking seems to satisfy all of my needs.

The idea for writing this book has been whirling around in my head for years, and always in the background there was one problem. I know that a cookbook should be full of recipes. But how can I put down recipes when I don't follow them exactly myself? Suddenly I realized what I do. I read a recipe and then I cook according to my instincts. The trick is, how does this process become a cookbook? So, I came up with a plan.

I am going to talk to you, my readers, as if you are standing next to me, and I'll take you through the adventures of everyday life with Bubby Irma.

First, you must understand that there are two basic ingredients in every recipe. These two ingredients set the mood of the day.

1. Love of food.
2. Love of the people you are cooking for.

If you leave out these two ingredients, cooking becomes a bore and a chore. If you include them, it can be a wonderful adventure.

Several years ago, my husband and I moved to the Jewish Quarter in Jerusalem's Old City. I soon realized that this was not just a place to live, but a way of life filled with exciting experiences and challenges. The Old City is steeped in history, but more than that, it fills one with awe.

Our apartment overlooks the Western Wall — the Kotel. As I look out my living room window, not only do I see people of our day wandering about, but I feel I am in the presence of our ancestors. Spiritual life has become a living truth.

With its many yeshivas and archeological centers, the Jewish Quarter has attracted students and tourists from all over the world. Artists are inspired to great heights, and fill the nooks and crannies of this historical place with their creative works. And young people, too, find inspiration here.

Our house is a haven for many yeshiva students. We have ten or twelve guests at our table every Friday night. It has become a challenge to cook with inspiration each time. How rewarding it is to have a young student finish a meal, recite the blessings, and then say "Irm, you did it again!"

My Family

We have three children. One daughter, Vicki, lives in Nairobi, Kenya, with her husband, Harold, and their daughters, Erika (now in Israel), Timna, and Andreia. Vicki became a *baalas teshuvah* when Timna was born thirteen years ago. They have lived in Kenya for ten years. It is not easy to keep a kosher home when you are the only one doing it. At first they lived as vegetarians — not by choice but out of necessity. Kenya, strange as it may sound, does have a wonderful Jewish community, and slowly they began to have more requests for kosher meats and other sundries, and were able to bring a *mashgiach* and a *shochet* to Nairobi to stock their freezers.

Today there almost 200 families in the Jewish community. More than 150 of them are Israeli families. They use a beautiful big synagogue built seventy-five years ago.

Vicki is very active in this community, and she is the chairperson for the Chevrah Kadisha (despite their small numbers, they do *taharas* by themselves.) The "House of Lopow" (my son-in-law's name) in Nairobi is the African annex to the "House of Charles." There, they create a little corner of Israel and Jewish suburbia, making their own famous potato knishes, bagels, homemade cream cheese and even "lox" (smoked Nile perch).

Vicki's oldest daughter, Erika, who is now nineteen,

decided that she wanted to live in Israel and become more religious. Four years ago, she came to Israel and decided to study in the girls' high school in Kfar Sava. She is now in her first year of college at Michlala.

Erika comes to our house every Shabbos. This is one of the miracles of living here. It is so wonderful having her around. For grandparents, this relationship represents a second chance. I could write a book on how to get along and enjoy your teenagers. I never criticize and I never say no; therefore we never have arguments!

Next is Debi, daughter number two. I really feel that she is responsible for making me aware of the miracles that happen. When we bought our apartment in the Jewish Quarter, Debi had been married for twelve years without having children. We met with many of the local rabbis, and Natie told them all about our Debi. They told us to advise our daughter to take on certain mitzvos.

Natie called her every week and nagged her about this. Her response was, "Daddy, have you joined the Jewish Moonies?" Finally, she gave in. About seven weeks later, we got a phone call from Debi—she didn't even say hello, just "I'm pregnant."

We had an overwhelming desire to thank Hashem for this wonderful gift. But how can you really thank Hashem? Only by living his ways and keeping his mitzvos. Natie started wearing a *kippah*, and we became *shomer Shabbos*. Several months later, we had a beautiful grandson, Aaron Michael, and he now has a sister, Elyse Michelle. Debi keeps a kosher home and is active in her synagogue. The children attend the Hebrew Academy in Silver Springs, Maryland.

The story of our son, Moshe, is another miracle that happened in the "House of Charles." Moshe made *aliyah* when he was fifteen years old, participating in the very first Youth Aliyah program from the U.S.A. He graduated high school in Israel, and when he was eighteen years old, right after the Yom Kippur War, he immediately joined the army. This was a completely voluntary act, because as a new immigrant he could have postponed his military service.

He spent three years with the paratroopers, and after that another year in the pilot training program.

Then he went to America to seek his fortune. Three years later he returned to Israel. Vicki was visiting us at the time and she talked Moshe into staying at Aish HaTorah Yeshiva for just three days (I think she actually bribed him into it.) After the first day, he decided to stay and study. Moshe was a very enthusiastic student. After studying at Aish HaTorah in Jerusalem, he received his *semichah* from Ner Yisrael in Baltimore.

Rabbi Matis Weinberg of Kerem Yeshiva became his mentor and they established a Torah relationship that continues in strength after nearly ten years. As well as becoming a rabbi, he learnt to be a *shochet*, a *mohel*, and a *sofer*. He wanted to have all the skills just in case he ever needed them.

Within a year of becoming a *baal teshuvah*, Moshe's rebbe, Rav Matis, and his wife Tziporah introduced him to Elana, a wonderful, beautiful girl from Oakland, California, and they were married soon afterwards. They now have a daughter, Shira, who is five years old. And lo and behold, all of Moshe's skills were put into use when he took the position of rabbi of the Nairobi Jewish Community.

You will also meet my sisters and brothers as you cook my recipes. There are no words to express how grateful I am to Hashem for placing me in such a special family. They are Helen, *a"h*, Mickey, Selma, *a"h*, and Herby. They all spoiled me — with love. I am who I am today because of them.

An Egg Is Not An Egg

The first year that we spent in the Old City was a year of learning and growing. It was at this time that we came to understand the true meaning of kashrus.

Before arriving in Israel, we were always active in our local synagogue, and we made our house kosher when our girls were sixteen and fourteen years old. We purchased new dishes, new silverware, and a new set of pots and pans.

A few days later, I went to my local Conservative rabbi with great enthusiasm and pride in what I was doing, and asked if he had any advice or help to give me. I had an overwhelming desire to do everything just right. He smiled and said, "Great, Irma. Here is a book. Read it,

and I am sure you will find all the answers you are looking for." I left his office disappointed. How could he have dismissed the matter so lightly?

I kept kosher — in spite of him. One day, I was happy to hear Vicki say, as she was reaching for a dish, "Mom, the best thing about keeping kosher is the realization that each time I reach for a milk dish or a meat dish, I am reinforcing my Judaism."

That is, I *thought* I kept kosher. It was only after I lived here in Jerusalem for a few weeks that I realized, not only wasn't I keeping kosher, but I really knew very little about Judaism. I began going to classes for women and found out just how little I did know.

One day, I was baking my famous Babka, and as I always did, I started to break the eggs into the dough. A little voice inside said, "No, no, I have to crack the eggs into a glass and check that there is no blood." If there was no blood, they could be used, but if there was, they were not to be eaten or used in a kosher kitchen.

I walked away from the dough and got a glass to crack the egg into. But I could not crack it. I heard a voice again: "Irma, you have been cooking for thirty-nine years and never cracked an egg into a glass

— it is ridiculous. Don't do it!" So I walked back to the dough and started to crack the egg. Again I was stopped by a voice that said, "Irma, if you are going to do something, do it right." So I cracked it into the glass, and what I saw and smelled put me in a state of shock. Not only was the egg rotten, but it was full of blood and even had a part of the beak formed. I dropped it and stood there in awe of Hashem. He had found a way to get his message across to me.

I told my experience to anyone and everyone who would listen. The yeshiva boys I was beginning to get to know loved the story, and one day while they were walking with the Rosh Yeshiva, they told him the story. He chuckled, and then he said, "Listen fellows, if she never knew about eggs, maybe you better check out her house to be sure it is kosher in case you ever want to eat there."

The boys came to me and asked if I would mind if they brought in a rabbi to kind of check out the house. I didn't mind at all — it was a good chance to learn something. That afternoon, the rabbi and two boys came into my house. They looked, asked questions about my dishes, and then went to the liquor cabinet. They put aside a box of all the liquors that were not kosher. The last bottle they condemned was Corvosier. I said, "Good, now Natie won't yell at me every time I use it in my mousse." The rabbi looked at me. "You cook with this ?" he asked. "Yes, but only when I make mousse." He gave a big sigh and said, "Fellows, I think you better *kasher* her pots, pans, and silverware."

Two evenings later, Steve and his friend came and started the kashering. We were up until 1 A.M. and we had to continue the next night. At 2 A.M. the last pot was finished. I was exhausted, but so glad to have it done and over with.

One last pot remained — the one that we had used for kashering the other pots. Steve and a friend took that pot over to a place where they had big vats of hot water, and kashered it there. They came back into the house and sat me down on the sofa to tell me that they were really sorry about all of the mess and work they had created, but unfortunately my house was still not kosher as I did not have enough knowledge of the laws. I could not believe my ears. What was all the work we had just done? What was the purpose of all of this? I became incensed, cried, and asked them to please leave my house.

The next day, I began to think about what had happened while I was cleaning up the mess, and I realized what they were saying and where they were coming from. They had in essence told me that we had done the kashering backwards. A person must know and understand the full concept of kashrus, its laws and reasons, if one is to maintain a kosher home. I finally heard what they had been trying to tell me. I got Steve from the Yeshiva and apologised for my show of anger. I asked him to please continue to come into our house — if only to sit at our table. He did.

After several weeks (during which time I learnt as much as I could about kashrus), I got up enough courage to invite a rabbi who was a very good friend of ours to come to have Shabbos lunch with us. He accepted.

Now came the challenge. I would make my first cholent. Again that big pot came in handy. I filled it with enough cholent to feed an army. I worked so hard on that meal. But when I got up early on Shabbos morning, I realized that I wasn't smelling anything cooking. Lo and behold — the oven was off! I had turned it too low, and the cholent never got cooked. (Lesson number one in making cholent: it must be fully cooked before putting it on the blech or in the oven to stay hot for Shabbos day. I learned the hard way.) I was frantic and went to all my neighbors to ask for their leftovers to serve.

We were fourteen for lunch at 10:30 A.M. The singing and *ruach* was so very special. I did put some of the raw cholent out and people took some, but no one asked for seconds.

When the boys learned that this rabbi had come to my house for a Shabbos meal, they started coming too. We often laugh and tease about it. We didn't know when we were well off — without all these boys coming we had so much less work to do!

Shabbos Starts on Wednesday

After a few weeks of feeling as if Shabbos were every other day, I realized that Shabbos actually starts on Wednesday for me. Shopping and baking take up the day. Thursday is soup and appetizer day, and Friday is major cooking and salad day. One thing I can never fathom: during the winter months, Shabbos comes in so early, about 4 P.M., and I am never ready—I always have to rush to get the last thing done—but in the summer, when Shabbos begins as late as 7 P.M.— I am still not ready. I

think I have a problem.

On Wednesday, I begin to feel the anticipation of the coming Shabbos. How many are coming? For which meal? What shall I serve? I begin to think about shopping and baking. If you ask my friends, they will laugh. "No way is Bubby Irma so organized." Mentally I am, it's just that somehow the day disappears and I still haven't done a thing. This is a clear case of "Do as I say, not as I do." It makes Thursday and Friday so much easier if you have something done on Wednesday. So, let's pretend that I am organized.

Let's start with cake and cookies. I usually begin with brownies, which I store away in a tin. Baking Apple Crisp and Oatmeal Crunchies on Wednesday is a disaster — by Friday, there is nothing left. The only way to save them is to hide them at the back of the freezer.

At this point, I also check my stock of homemade pickles and make more if necessary. With my instant pickle recipe, you can add more cucumbers, garlic, and either lemon juice or vinegar at any time. I usually make a new batch once a month.

Thursday morning is the best time to shop in the Old City — all the produce is fresh then. I defrost the chickens and bake the potato knishes, a Yerushalmi kugel for Shabbos lunch, and perhaps a vegetable quiche. I like to have all my desserts made by Thursday evening, so dinner on Thursday night has to be the simplest and easiest of the week. If I am lucky, I get Natie to take us out to dinner. If I have been lazy on Wednesday, I must make the dessert Thursday evening.

Thursday is a perfect time to make Gefilte Fish. Rice and Ratatouille can be made on Friday, along with the chicken soup and Mocca Garlic Chicken. This unusual chicken recipe is not only easy to make, but the compliments it brings put you on a high for the evening. Finish off the meal with warm Apple Crisp topped with a serving of Parve Ice Cream.

On Thursday I also check and soak the beans and peel the potatoes ready to be cooked on Friday.

Bright and early Friday morning, Natie makes the challah dough and cuts up the chickens. As the dough is rising, I begin to make the chicken soup, reserving parts of the chickens for the main dish. I put two big pots on the stove, one filled with water for the soup and one for the sauce that the main-dish chicken will be cooked in.

I have discovered a surefire way to avoid cleaning the chickens, and it is even healthier. Natie skins them as he is cutting them up, so all I have to clean are the wings. The soup is cooked for one hour and then removed from the fire until an hour before Shabbos when Natie or I test and adjust the seasoning and finish cooking.

Now it is time to punch down the challah dough and let it rise once again to double its size which takes about an hour or more. When the dough is ready, I knead in the raisins and braid the challahs. Then I carefully place them on cookie sheets and brush on the egg wash (I use either the yolk with a bit of water added or, to save on cholesterol, just the whites — either one will give the challah a shiny brown gloss.) Now I set them aside to rise once more before baking.

At this stage, I must give some thought to the menu for Shabbos day. Recently, Natie and I realized that three full Shabbos meals are just too much food for our aging systems. So, at least one of our meals is just symbolic; we break bread together and perhaps have a bowl of soup. However, if we have guests I always make a proper lunch.

A traditional cholent is the main course of the winter Shabbos lunch. Salads, cold chicken, and, of course, a Yerushalmi kugel round out the meal.

Now, the "third meal" has to be planned. It has become a social event in the House of Charles. We never know who is coming, or how many. So I just set the table for lots of people and make it an easy dinner. In the winter, it is a parve meal, because it comes so close after the meat lunch. This is not always easy, but there are several recipes that I have discovered or invented for this meal. Tomato pie, spinach knish, or potato knish are all ideal. In summertime, when Shabbos doesn't end till around 8 o' clock, I serve a cheese quiche with two or three salads prepared on Friday.

By this time, the kitchen looks like a cyclone has hit it. I am a fast, good cook, but neatness was never one of my attributes. However, I finally came up with a great solution: I call Miriam, my friend's daughter, to come in to clean the kitchen and set the table for Shabbos. (And when Erika is home from school, *she* gets the pleasure of cleaning the kitchen and setting the table for Shabbos.)

When she leaves, the house begins to look and smell like Shabbos. The silver gleams, the table is beautiful, and there is an aura fit for welcoming the Shabbos Queen.

Enter the Sabbath Queen

The Shabbos siren goes off, I light my candles, and Natie leaves for evening services. The next hour and a half are the most precious ninety minutes of my entire week. I relax in the living room, enjoying the peace and quiet, and the unique atmosphere of Shabbos in Jerusalem that must be experienced at least once in your life.

The dinner guests arrive, and we begin to feel the

serenity of the hour. Natie makes Kiddush and then we all wash our hands before partaking of the challah. (I usually try to keep the bread warm—it is so delicious.) Natie makes the *berachah* and takes a bite. We all hold

our breath and wait for his comments. Is it good this week? Are there enough raisins? Is it sweet enough? Finally, he smiles and says, "Pretty good — in fact, real good. This is a good one." I sigh with relief and get on with serving dinner. This has become such a ritual that the newly married yeshiva boys have begun to make challahs and imitate Natie in their homes.

Between courses, the men at the table sing *zemiros* (Shabbos songs). Just before the dessert is served, one of the Yeshiva boys gives us a *devar Torah*. What is a *devar Torah?* I actually struggled with this one for a long time, but one day I understood. It is a mini-lecture, given in order to understand the Torah portion that will be read on Shabbos morning.

When we have all finished with dessert, we begin *bentching*, thanking Hashem for the food that we have just eaten. In my house, we have a beautiful tune for this prayer.

Before the evening ends, more of the Yeshiva boys stop over for dessert or just to wish us a "*Shabbat shalom.*"

Shabbos morning is very special. Natie has established a tradition of going to services at Toras Chaim synagogue in the Moslem Quarter of the Old City. This synagogue has a dramatic and unusual story to it. Toras Chaim was the only synagogue left standing during the Arab occupation of the Old City. It was guarded by an Arab family who lived on the bottom floor of the building. The story goes that the father once attempted to break the walls that hid the Torah scrolls of the shul. He raised his hatchet, but suddenly his arm couldn't move. He tried again and again, and could not get his arm to come down on the wall. His son also tried, but his arm would not move either. At last, in total fear and awe, the men retreated.

After the city was liberated, the father told this tale to the men who came back to the synagogue. The men who daven at Toras Chaim have a strong connection with the shul. Most of them were bar mitzvahed there, and now more weddings and bar mitzvahs bring joy and laughter back to this very special place.

When Natie comes home, we go to a kiddush at our next-door neighbors', the Wallises. It is a standing joke between us that we really need this kiddush. Why? It is difficult to understand, but without the kiddush, we would not see each other for weeks. The week flies by, and we never seem to catch up with one another.

After kiddush, we take a walk, have our lunch, relax, and read until we fall blissfully asleep for our Shabbos nap. Heaven help the person who wakes us!

When we are invited out for Shabbos, Natie is always ready to go, but I find that there is something left undone — somehow my week is incomplete. So, I start planning for next Shabbos.

Shabbos has put tranquility into my life. The world stops moving, and I get off. It is time to relax, enjoy our friendships, and study Torah. The rabbis here in the Old City give wonderful classes on Shabbos. Rabbi Nachman Kahane gives a wonderful class in his synagogue. It's amazing how Natie wakes up from his Shabbos nap and runs to the class. I often join him and come home with a renewed dedication to Torah and mitzvos.

From Thursday evening, we begin greeting people with a warm "*Shabbat shalom*" — have a peaceful Shabbos, and just after Havdalah we greet them with "*Shavua tov*" — have a good week.

On Sunday I have renewed energy, and I am fortified to face the everyday trials and tribulations, knowing that Shabbos will soon be here again.

*   *   *

Because I live in a very special house in a very special city, I want to share it all with you. From time to time I will insert little stories about the recipes and I will try to recapture some of the wonderful pieces of life here for you to enjoy.

*   *   *

One very important piece of advice to my readers: cooking is fun and you can make it fun. Do not be afraid to trust your taste buds and alter seasonings to your taste. Use all basic recipes as a guide to produce the kind of food you enjoy.

A Note from Bubby about Measurements

Because I live in Israel, I usually cook in kilos! I have converted my recipes to pounds and ounces for my American readers. If you want to convert back to metric, feel free to substitute

1/2 kg. for 1 lb.

25 gms. for 1 oz.

2.5 cms. for 1 inch

4 cups for 1 quart

Oven temperatures are in Fahrenheit.

BREADS and BISCUITS

When we first moved to Israel back in 1972, bagels were not to be found, lox was unheard of, and smoked whitefish did not exist. Cream cheese at its best tasted like plaster. How could a full-bred Jewish American Princess live without these delicacies? This became a challenge.

I discovered that I could simulate fish to taste like lox. However, it was a week-long process, remembering to turn it every day. For me it was just too much of a patchka (bother). My cooking has to be fast and easy. I make last-minute decisions on what to eat, and planning a week ahead just never fit into my busy schedule.

Israel, being the progressive country that it is, eventually put a smoked salmon on the market. Now all I needed was the bagel and cream cheese to go with it. I tried many many recipes for bagels, and this is the one I like best.

Bagels

2 oz. dry or fresh **yeast**

2 cups warm **water**

3 Tbsp. **sugar**

3 tsp. **salt**

5½ – 6 cups **flour**

3 quarts **water** plus 1 Tbsp. **sugar**

cornmeal

1 **egg yolk** with 1 Tbsp. **water**

Dissolve yeast in 2 cups warm water. Stir in sugar and salt plus 4 cups flour. Beat well to make a smooth batter. Mix in ¼ cup more flour to make a stiff dough.

Turn dough out onto floured board. Knead for 10 – 15 minutes. (Using an electric beater with dough hook, knead 3 minutes only.) Add more flour if needed — dough should be harder than usual. Turn over in a greased bowl and let rise about 40 minutes.

Punch down and knead for 3 minutes. Roll portions of dough into a rectangle — it must not be a thin dough — about 1" thick, and then cut circles out with a large glass and punch a hole in with your fingers, twirling it around to form a circle (use the two index fingers). Continue until all the dough has been used. Let stand lightly covered — about 20 minutes.

Another method is to form a roll about 3" thick and cut slices off to twirl around your fingers.

Bring 3 quarts of water plus 1 Tbsp. sugar to a boil and carefully put bagels into the boiling water — about 5 or 6 at a time, depending on the size of the pot. Let bagels cook 5 minutes and lift out with a slotted spoon. Place bagels on a cookie sheet that has been sprinkled with cornmeal. After all bagels are boiled and on the cookie sheets, brush them with egg yolk mixture. Bake at 400° for 20 – 30 minutes.

VARIATION

I have discovered still another way to use this dough. Roll pieces of the dough into strips about 8" long and shape them into pretzels. After they are boiled and the egg yolk is brushed on, dip the pretzel into salt (I use kashering salt) and bake them in a medium oven until they are done. You now have Soft Pretzels. Serve with mustard.

Challah

1/2 cup **oil**

1/2 cup **honey**

1 Tbsp. **salt**

3 **eggs**

2 cups warm **water**

2 oz. fresh or dried **yeast**

8 – 9 cups **flour** (whole wheat and white — a combination of both flours makes the best challahs)

Mix ingredients, putting oil into the bowl first, and then measuring and adding honey, using the same measuring cup that you measured the oil in. This little trick allows the honey to run smoothly out of the measuring cup. Add remaining ingredients in order given.

Yeast can be purchased in two forms: fresh, solid cubes and yeast granules. I use yeast granules, and these dissolve well mixed into the recipe just before flour is added. If you use fresh yeast, dissolve it in 1 cup of the warm water before putting it into the bowl.

When making my challah in an electric mixer, I let it knead for 3 minutes and then do a little hand kneading as I transfer the dough into an oiled bowl. If it is kneaded by hand, it is necessary to knead the dough for 10 minutes.

Let dough rise in a large bowl that has been coated with oil. When transferring dough into the oiled bowl, be sure to turn it on all sides so that it gets a thin coating of oil. Place the bowl in a warm place covered with a towel until dough is double in size, then punch down and knead a bit more.

Place dough back in the bowl and let it rise a second time. This should take about one hour. Punch down and cut into sizes desired. When the breads are shaped, brush them immediately with egg yolk (so bread doesn't flatten from brushing) and sprinkle either poppy seeds or sesame seeds on the loaves. Let rise for another 20 minutes.

Bake at 350° for approx. 25 – 30 minutes or until challah sounds hollow when tapped on the bottom. This recipe makes four evenly divided challahs or one large one and two medium. I have also made it into one large challah for *sheva brachos* or special occasions.

THE CHALLAH STORY

Until we moved to Israel, my breads came out of the bakery. However, the first time I made my own challah, I was hooked. There is such joy and satisfaction when you bring a beautiful homemade challah to the Shabbos table.

It was a huge success, and each time I went back to the States to see my children and family, I had strict orders from my daughter. "Mom, you know you can't go back to Israel without filling the freezer with challahs." And, of course, I did just that.

A few years ago, Natie had to go to the States without me. I persuaded him that he could make challahs for the kids and surprise them. He wrote the recipe in his date book and did just that. When he came back, there was no living with him. He was so proud of "his challahs" that I lost my job, and now he makes the challahs every Friday morning before he goes to study at the Yeshiva, and I braid and bake them.

Challahs for Large Parties

13 cups **flour** (preferably 9 cups whole wheat and 4 cups white)

2 oz. **yeast**

1 Tbsp. **sugar**

1 cup **warm water**

1 cup **brown sugar**

2 Tbsp. **salt**

1 cup **oil**

3 **eggs**

Spread 1 Tbsp. sugar over yeast in warm water. The yeast will activate and form bubbles. Sprinkle one cup brown sugar onto flour (white sugar or honey can also be used). Make a well in flour and add rest of ingredients. Additional water may be added until dough is the right consistency, slightly sticky to the hand. Knead for 10 minutes vigorously by hand, or knead for 3 minutes in an electric mixer. Let rise in a warm place until double in size. Punch down and let rise once more. Cut dough into as many breads as you want to make. Many people like to make and freeze their challahs.

Pumpernickel Raisin Bread

1½ cups lukewarm **water**

½ cup **molasses**

2 oz. dry **yeast**

1 Tbsp. **instant coffee** granules

1 Tbsp. **salt**

2 cups **medium rye flour**

2 cups **whole wheat flour**

2 cups **all-purpose flour**

1½ Tbsp. **cocoa powder**

2 Tbsp. **oil**

1 cup **raisins**

cornmeal to spread on baking tin

1 **egg white**

1 Tbsp. cold **water**

Mix water, molasses, and yeast together, and stir to dissolve yeast. Let stand for 10 minutes—it will become foamy. Stir in coffee, rye flour, whole wheat flour, 1 cup all-purpose flour, cocoa, and salt. Dough should be sticky. If it is too sticky, add a little more all-purpose flour.

Turn bread onto a floured work surface and let it rest. Sprinkle some flour over dough and knead until smooth and elastic. It will still feel sticky.

Pour oil into a bowl and turn dough around in it until completely covered with oil. Cover dough and set aside to rise till triple in size — 3 – 4 hours.

Turn dough onto lightly floured work surface and flatten it into a large rectangle. Sprinkle with raisins. Knead dough for about 8 minutes. Let rise in bowl until double its size. This should take about 1 hour. Sprinkle baking sheet with cornmeal.

Turn bread out and cut into 3 pieces. Shape each piece into round loaves and set them on the baking sheet. Brush loaves with egg white that has been mixed with water. Let rise until doubled.

Preheat oven to 400°. Bake for 35 – 45 minutes or until breads are dark brown and sound hollow when the bottoms are rapped. Cool completely before cutting.

On Purim there is a custom of exchanging gifts with our neighbors and friends. One year I made about twenty-five small pumpernickel breads and put them into my Purim treats. They were a huge success.

Basic Whole Grain Bread

3 cups **warm water**

1 Tbsp. **brown sugar**

1 Tbsp. **dry yeast**

5 cups **whole wheat flour**

1 cup **white flour**

1 Tbsp. **salt**

Pour warm water into a bowl. Add sugar and sprinkle yeast on top. When it becomes bubbly, add half the flour and beat well until the dough ceases to be grainy and becomes smooth and stretchy.

Add salt and remaining flour — 1 cup at a time — kneading until it is no longer sticky. Turn dough out onto a floured board.

As dough gets stiffer and harder to knead, sprinkle remaining flour on tabletop and knead dough on top of it.

After kneading dough, put it into a greased bowl and cover it. Let it rise in a warm, draft-free place until it becomes double in size. Punch down dough and shape into loaves and put into greased pans. (I use loaf pans and make two loaves.) Cover and let loaves double in size —

they should fill pan when doubled.

Preheat oven to 375º. When bread is rounded above rim of pan, bake for 40 minutes.

The bread should be a rich golden brown and have a slightly hollow sound when tapped.

Erika discovered this bread and she makes it when she has time off from school. She is a wonderful cook and loves making up and trying new recipes.

Carrot Coconut Bread

2½ cups **flour**

1 cup **sugar or** substitute ¾ cup **apple juice concentrate**

1 tsp. **baking powder**

1 tsp. **cinnamon**

½ tsp. **salt**

3 **eggs**

½ cup **oil**

½ cup **water**

2 cups shredded **carrots**

1½ cups **coconut**

½ cup **raisins**

½ cup **pecans**

chopped **dried apricots** (optional)

Mix flour, sugar, baking powder, cinnamon, and salt together. Beat eggs, and add oil and water into batter. Fold in remaining ingredients.

Pour into two loaf pans, or a 9" x 13" rectangular pan. Bake at 350° for 45 minutes.

HINT: *Do not let it overbake!!! If this should happen, just pour apple juice or orange juice over the bread as it comes out of the oven and cover with a towel. This will keep it moist.*

Apricot Bread

1 cup **dried apricots**

2 cups **whole wheat flour**

3 tsp. **baking powder**

¼ tsp. **salt**

1 cup **brown sugar**

4 Tbsp. **butter or margarine**

2 **eggs**, beaten

½ cup **orange juice**

¼ cup **water**

½ cup chopped **nuts**

Soak apricots in warm water for 30 minutes. Drain and cut in pieces with scissors. Sift flour, baking powder, and salt together. Cream sugar and butter, and add beaten eggs. Add dry ingredients alternately with orange juice and water. Add chopped nuts and apricots. Bake in greased loaf pan, lined on bottom with waxed paper, at 350° for 50 – 55 minutes.

Banana Bread

2½ cups **sugar** (less if bananas are very sweet)

8 oz. **butter or margarine**

4 **eggs**

2 tsp. **baking soda**

8 Tbsp. **sour cream or parve whip**

4 – 6 ripe **bananas**

3 cups **flour** (whole wheat or white or mixed)

2 tsp. **vanilla**

chopped **nuts**

Mix all ingredients in an electric mixer and bake in loaf pans at 350° for 40 – 45 minutes. The trick to this is to keep the bread moist by underbaking it.

VARIATION

Use 1 cup **apple juice concentrate or** ¼ cup **orange juice concentrate** instead of sugar.

This alternative works well and is great for dieters who need a dessert but cannot tolerate sugar.

HINT: If you find that you have baked it too long, orange juice or apple juice may be poured over the hot bread. Covering it with a towel lets the moisture stay in.

After personally going through hundreds of diet schemes, I have found that the first step is to eliminate sugar from my system. Even one small taste can start me back on an eating binge.

Quick Applesauce Bread

2 cups **whole wheat flour**, sifted

½ tsp. **baking soda**

1 tsp. **baking powder**

½ tsp. **salt**

4 oz. **butter or margarine**

¾ cup **brown sugar**

2 **eggs**, well-beaten

3 Tbsp. **buttermilk, sour milk or parve cream**

1 medium-sized **apple**, grated, plus enough **applesauce** to make 1 cup

Sift dry ingredients together twice. Cream butter and sugar. Add eggs, sour milk, and applesauce mixture. Add dry ingredients and blend well. Bake in greased loaf pan at 350° – 375° for 1 hour.

Date and Nut Bread

4 Tbsp. **margarine**

1 cup pitted **dates**

¼ cup **brown sugar or** ¼ cup **apple juice concentrate**

¼ cup **white sugar**

¾ cup boiling **water**

1 **egg**, beaten

2 cups all-purpose **flour** (sifted) **or whole wheat flour**

2 tsp. **baking powder**

½ tsp. **salt**

½ cup chopped **nuts**

½ tsp. **vanilla**

1½ tsp. **rum** (optional)

Place margarine, dates, and both sugars in a bowl. Pour boiling water over ingredients. Let sit for 8 minutes and stir well. Cool, add egg, and mix. Add flour, baking powder, and salt to mixture and beat for 1 minute. Fold in nuts and vanilla, and rum if using. Pour into a loaf pan.
Bake at 350° for 50 – 60 minutes.

Scones

3 cups **self-rising flour** plus 1 tsp. **baking powder or** 3 cups **regular or whole wheat flour** plus 2 tsp. **baking powder**

8 oz. **margarine**

pinch of **salt**

6 Tbsp. **sugar**

8 oz. **milk**

½ cup **raisins**

Mix everything together. Roll out to a very thick dough and cut circles with a glass—size is up to you — or shape the scones in your hands. You should get about 12 scones. Bake at 450° for 15 minutes.

My Yeshiva boys love scones. I once made the mistake of making a batch of scones for a special treat. Now there is just no way I can get out of making them at least once a month. The favorite line here when one of the boys stops in is, "It smells so good in here. Are you baking scones?" How can I refuse?

Pecan Orange Bread

2 **eggs**, separated

4 oz. **margarine**

¾ cup **sugar or** ½ cup **apple juice concentrate or orange juice concentrate**

grated **rind** of 1 **orange**

1½ cups **flour**

1½ tsp. **baking powder**

¼ tsp. **baking soda**

¼ tsp. **salt**

½ cup fresh **orange juice**

1 cup chopped **pecans**

Beat egg whites and set aside. Cream margarine and sugar until light and fluffy. Beat in egg yolks one at a time, then grated orange rind. Sift flour, baking powder, baking soda, and salt together. Add ½ cup orange juice. Fold in nuts and egg whites. Pour into a loaf pan and bake at 350° for 50 – 60 minutes.

Prune Bread

2 cups sifted **whole wheat flour**

½ tsp. **salt**

2½ tsp. **baking powder**

½ tsp. **baking soda**

½ cup **brown sugar**

½ cup **oil**

1 **egg**, well beaten

1 cup **quick-cooking oatmeal**

1 cup **buttermilk or parve cream**

¾ cup pitted, cooked, chopped **prunes**

½ cup chopped **walnuts** (optional)

Sift first 4 dry ingredients. Cream sugar and oil. Add egg and oatmeal. Add sifted ingredients alternately with liquids. Pour batter into a loaf pan and bake at 250° – 350° for 70 – 80 minutes.

HINT: *A sugar substitute can be used for the weight-conscious.*

Zucchini Bread

3 Tbsp. **margarine**

3 **eggs**

1¼ cups **oil**

1½ cups **sugar or** 7/8 cup **apple juice concentrate**

1 tsp. **vanilla**

2 cups grated **zucchini**

2 cups all-purpose **flour**

2 tsp. **baking soda**

1 tsp. **baking powder**

1 tsp. **salt**

1 tsp. ground **cinnamon**

1 tsp. ground **cloves**

1 cup chopped **nuts**

Beat eggs, oil, margarine, sugar, and vanilla until light and thick. Fold in grated zucchini. Stir sifted dry ingredients into mixture and fold in nuts. Pour into two 9" x 5" loaf pans and bake at 350° for 45 minutes or until cake tester comes out clean. Cool before removing bread from pan.

APPETIZERS

Chopped Eggs

7 – 9 hard-boiled **eggs**

1 medium **onion**, chopped fine

1 – 2 Tbsp. **chicken fat or margarine or oil**

¼ tsp. **garlic powder**

Chop all ingredients together and serve individual servings on a bed of lettuce.

VARIATION

This recipe can be used for Egg Salad by substituting mayonnaise for chicken fat.

Chopped Liver

1 large **onion**

½ lb. fresh **mushrooms**

1 clove **garlic**

3 Tbsp. **olive oil**

3 – 4 **hard-boiled eggs**

12 oz. **broiled liver**

In a food processor, chop onion, mushrooms, and garlic. Heat olive oil in a frying pan and add onion, mushroom, and garlic. Fry until brown. Process eggs. Process or chop liver separately. Mix all ingredients together. Add 1 extra Tbsp. olive oil. Salt and pepper to taste.

HINT: *For Chopped Liver to taste like Bubby's used to, use chicken fat instead of olive oil.*

Grilled Eggplant Spread with Coriander

When barbecuing, after having removed the meat or chicken from the charcoal grill, it is possible to put on an eggplant or two to cook so you can make a spread for the next day. If eggplant is grilled until it is very tender, you do not have to bother with removing the skin before pureeing it. The spread will have a dark hue and a pleasing smoky taste. Of course, the eggplant can always be grilled in the oven.

1 fairly large **eggplant** (about 1 lb.)

1 – 2 Tbsp. best quality **olive oil**

1 large clove **garlic**

2 Tbsp. small **coriander sprigs**

salt and **pepper**

tomato slices and **coriander sprigs** for garnish

Prick eggplant a few times. Grill over coals or in a broiler, turning often, for 45 minutes or until tender. Cool. Cut off the end. Remove skin.

Puree eggplant in food processor. Pour in olive oil. Add garlic and coriander, and process again. Season to taste with salt and pepper. To serve, garnish with tomato slices and coriander sprigs.

Artichokes

1 **artichoke** per person

6 **bay leaves**

salt and **pepper** to taste

2 oz. **butter or margarine**

fresh or powdered **garlic**

Cut stems short and boil artichokes in a large pot with enough water to cover them, together with seasoning, until a leaf can be pulled out easily — about 30 minutes.

Melt butter and add garlic. Place this sauce beside each plate, and your guests can pull the leaves off and dip the bottoms into the sauce, eating just the bottom of the leaves. When the heart of the artichoke is reached, cut out the choke and eat the succulent meat dipped in the sauce.

Sweet and Sour Fish

slices of **carp, pike, or Nile perch** (amount to be determined by number of guests you expect)

1 large **onion**

1 **carrot**

1/2 tsp. **salt**

dash of **pepper**

1 **parsley root** (optional)

pickling mixture

1/2 cup **brown sugar**

2 **bay leaves**

3 cloves **garlic**

salt to taste

dash of **pepper**, **nutmeg**, and **allspice**

juice of 1 whole **lemon**

1/2 cup **vinegar**

1/2 cup **water**

Put everything into a pot and cover with water to at least 1" above the ingredients. Bring to a boil and cook for 15 minutes. Taste and add more sugar or salt, if needed.

A FISH STORY

Making gefilte fish is a challenge. My mother made it, my grandmother made it, and I had to make it. In order to become a real balabusta (woman of the house), I had to prove myself in the kitchen. Challah, chicken soup, and gefilte fish had to be made successfully, and then you knew you were on the way to becoming a balabusta. The first time I made it, I was so proud. But, like every child, I needed my parents' approval. At that time we were living in Worcester, Mass., and my parents lived in Camden, New Jersey. I decided to do what my sister Helen did — she had lilacs in her garden, and they were among my mother's favorite flowers. Each year she took the first cuttings and wrapped them well and sent them from Washington, D.C., to my mother in New Jersey.

I carefully wrapped a jar of the freshly made delicacy and sent it out air mail, special delivery. (This was before overnight delivery service.) A few days later I received a call from Mom and Dad telling me how great the fish was. I was thrilled. Years later, they finally told me the truth...it arrived spoiled, but they didn't want to hurt my feelings. I made another batch while they were visiting and got their full approval.

Gefilte Fish

2 **carrots**

1 large **onion**

½ cup **water**

1 raw **egg**

½ cup **matzah meal**

1 tsp. **salt**

1 Tbsp. **sugar**

½ tsp. **pepper**

2 lb. fresh ground **fish**—either carp or a mixture of carp, whitefish, and/or pike. Nile perch is a new addition to our list of fishes — it is used alone.

Grind together all ingredients, and then mix in ground fish. At this point the fish may be formed into logs — approx. 3" wide and 12" long — wrapped tightly in tin foil for freezing. To cook, just remove foil from frozen fish logs and drop into boiling sauce. It is easy to slice for individual servings. Or, form ovals about the size of a pear. Drop them into boiling sauce and allow to cook slowly for 2 hours. Let cool before removing fish balls from sauce. Serve with horseradish on a bed of lettuce. A slice of cooked carrot adds color to the dish.

Cooking Sauce

4 cups **water**

4 **carrots**, sliced

3 **onions**, sliced

1 Tbsp. **salt** and 1 tsp. **pepper**

2 Tbsp. **sugar**

fish bones and **heads**

Bring everything to a boil and add fish balls or logs.

Seviche (Mexican Fish)

1½ lbs. **fillet of sole**

½ cup **lemon or lime juice**

Remove any skin from fillets and cut fish into thin strips. Place them in a deep porcelain or glass bowl. The juice should cover the fish — add more if necessary. Leave in refrigerator to marinate for 3 – 4 hours.

Sauce

4 Tbsp. **olive oil**

2 medium **tomatoes**, diced

fresh **chili pepper** (optional)

1 **onion**, chopped

2 Tbsp. chopped **parsley**

½ tsp. **oregano**

salt and **pepper** to taste

Mix together sauce ingredients and pour over fish. Serve on a bed of lettuce.

Salmon Mousse

1 lb. **cream cheese**

1 large can **salmon**

1 Tbsp. **horseradish**

½ tsp. **lemon juice**

walnuts

chopped **parsley**

Mix all ingredients except walnuts and parsley, and form a ball. Roll ball into the walnuts and parsley. Serve with crackers.

Mock Chopped Liver

1 **onion**, chopped

2 cans **green beans**, drained, **or** 2 lb. **fresh green beans**, cooked

⅓ cup **walnuts**

3 pieces **black bread or pumpernickel**

3 **hard-boiled eggs**

Sauté onion. Place all ingredients in food processor with the steel blade. Chop until desired consistency is reached. I actually like it on the coarse side. Salt and pepper to taste.

I have found that fresh green beans are much tastier. When I am not able to get them, I use fresh or frozen broccoli or peas.

Mushroom and Spinach Florentine

1 lb. **mushrooms**, sliced

1 medium **onion**, diced

2 pkgs. **frozen spinach**, thawed

1 tsp. **salt**

$1/4$ **onion**, chopped

1 **egg**

1 heaping Tbsp. **mushroom soup mix**
     or 1 can **cream of mushroom soup**

garlic

2 oz. **butter or margarine**, melted

1 cup grated **cheddar cheese**

Sauté mushrooms and onion until brown. Line 10" x 15" casserole with half the spinach, salt, egg, mushroom soup, chopped onion, and butter or margarine. Sprinkle with half the cheese and mushrooms. Repeat with remainder of ingredients — top layer being cheese. Bake at 350° for 20 minutes.

Stuffed Mushrooms

1 lb. **mushrooms**

1 **onion**, chopped

1 clove **garlic,** crushed

1 Tbsp. oil

$1/2$ cup fine **breadcrumbs**

chopped **parsley**

salt and **pepper** to taste

Remove stems from mushrooms, leaving caps to be used for stuffing. Sauté onion and mushroom stems with garlic in oil. Add breadcrumbs and chopped parsley. Season to taste. Use a teaspoon to fill mushroom caps with stuffing.

These delicacies may be either baked in a medium oven on a cookie sheet or steamed on top of the stove. I have best results in the oven. Stuffed mushrooms do take a little time to prepare, but the end results make it a special treat.

A Meatball Story

Each time I prepare this easy, delicious recipe I think of the first time I ate it. My sister Selma was a wonderful cook — and she set a table that made her delicious food even more appetizing. I first became interested in cooking at a family party that Selma had at her house. The meatballs were the rave of the day.

The Lieberman family was a large and very close, but competitive family. We always loved getting together with our aunts and uncles. To get a rise out of them, all you had to do was ask any one of them his age. Each year they seemed to get younger, and listening to them argue about their ages was the entertainment of the day.

They were all good cooks. When the younger generation, my contemporaries, started having meetings at their homes we all went out of our way to make food that we could be proud of, and this meatball recipe took top honors.

Sweet and Sour Meatballs

2 lbs. **chopped beef, chopped chicken, or chopped turkey**

1 large or 2 small **potatoes**

1 large **onion**

lots of **garlic**

Sauce

1 14 oz. bottle **ketchup** (hot or regular)

1 ketchup bottle of **water**

1 heaping Tbsp. **brown sugar**

Grate potatoes, onion, and garlic into chopped meat and form balls. Drop balls into sauce and cook for 1 hour.

Knishes

My recipe for Potato Knishes is one of my favorites and it's always successful. I did not invent this recipe, but I have done so many different things with it that I continually thank Tziporah Weinberg for introducing me to this delicacy.

I have much more than that to thank Tziporah for. She and Rabbi Matis Weinberg gave my son his wife, Elana. The Weinbergs have a beautiful family. I am always amazed at how enjoyable it is to have Shabbos with them and watch the interaction of the entire family. Sometimes it gets a bit hectic, but no one cares — the food that goes on that table is food for the soul. Good, unusually tasty and always too much.

This is a recipe that can be varied, giving one the satisfaction of creativity. Your guests will shriek with joy after the first taste. I use this as a special appetizer and make sure that I have enough for seconds.

If I find that I don't have a package of puff pastry in the freezer, I make my own dough, which is a simple piecrust.

Dough

2 cups **flour**

pinch of **salt**

8 oz. **margarine**

HAND METHOD:
Mix flour, salt, and margarine until it forms tiny crumbs. Gradually add ice water until dough forms a solid ball. Refrigerate for 20 minutes.

PROCESSOR METHOD:
Cut margarine into smaller pieces. Add flour and salt. Process until it looks like small pebbles. Add 3 – 6 tsp. ice water while processor is running and stop when dough forms a ball. Remove and let rest in refrigerator for 20 – 30 minutes. (If I am in a hurry, I often put dough in freezer for 10 – 15 minutes.)

Roll dough out into a rectangle — I usually get two rectangles out of either choice of dough. To use prepared dough, cut package in half. A floured board aids in the rolling. Place filling in middle of rectangle and fold right side of the dough over it. Place another line of filling on top and fold left side over. This makes a long roll to be placed on a well-greased cookie sheet and washed with egg. Slit the roll halfway through at 2" intervals. Make second roll and bake at 350° for 30 minutes or until dough is browned on top and solid-looking.

Potato Filling

6 – 8 potatoes, depending on size

2 **onions**, chopped

salt and **pepper**

garlic, chopped

oil

Boil potatoes until soft. Fry onions and garlic in oil until transparent. Mash potatoes with onion mixture and season to taste.

I often use leftover meats mashed with the potatoes. A vegetable filling for the vegetarians in the crowd is always a welcome dish. For this delicious treat, I use all types of leftover vegetables. Fry onions and garlic, and chop vegetables in food processor. Mix with fried onions and garlic—filling should have consistency of the mashed potato filling. Spinach and cream cheese filling for a dairy meal with a tossed salad makes this a special luncheon treat.

The knishes in themselves are delicious, but served with a wine, garlic, and mushroom sauce they become a gourmet delight.

Sauce

1 **onion**

1 clove **garlic**

1 cup fresh or canned **mushrooms**

1 large Tbsp. **mushroom soup mix or** 1 Tbsp. **cornstarch** dissolved in water

1 cup **water**

$1/2$ – 1 cup **white wine**

Chop and sauté onion and garlic. Add mushrooms and water. Simmer for 3 minutes, then add mushroom soup mix. Allow sauce to thicken and add white wine. Serve over each slice of knish. The soup mix can be left out — in that case, use either cornstarch or flour to thicken the sauce.

This sauce is what makes the difference —— it puts the knish right into the "Gourmet" class.

Fruits

On a hot summer night I often serve just fruit for an appetizer — either a fruit salad or melon. Each fruit in its season is succulent and delicious. Fruit and vegetables here in Israel have very special flavors. Our produce is not picked and put into cold storage — it is picked and then bought by the vendor who resells it to the housewife. Often in a matter of hours it is served at our table.

In the soup section you will find many cold soups and fruit soups that make delightful appetizers.

SALADS

Marinated Cabbage Salad

1 head **cabbage**, shredded medium

2 **cucumbers**, sliced

3 **carrots**, sliced

1 **onion**, sliced

Marinade

¾ cup **vinegar**

½ cup **sugar or honey** (even better)

½ cup **oil** (can be omitted)

4 tsp. **salt**

Mix marinade ingredients and pour over tossed vegetables. It can be stored in the refrigerator for at least one week. To freshen it up, just add fresh crisp cabbage.

A tip for dieters: use sugar substitute and add fresh lemon juice.

VARIATION
Add green and/or red peppers.

Beet and Pineapple Salad

4 or 5 **beets**, cooked

1 20 oz. can **pineapple chunks**, drained

chopped **walnuts**

2 – 3 Tbsp. **mayonnaise**

Cut beets into cubes and add rest of ingredients. Marinate for 1 hour before serving.

Caesar Salad

4 cloves **garlic**

1/4 cup **olive oil**

1 cup **breadcrumbs**

1/4 cup regular **oil**

1 **egg**

juice of 1/2 **lemon**

1/2 tsp. **salt**

1/4 tsp. **dry mustard**

1/4 tsp. **pepper**

1 1/2 tsp. **Worcestershire sauce**

1 can **anchovies**, drained and chopped

1/4 cup **blue cheese**

2 Tbsp. grated **Parmesan cheese**

1 head **lettuce** (iceberg or romaine)

croutons

Crush garlic and add olive oil. Refrigerate 1 hour. Mix breadcrumbs with 2 Tbsp. of the regular oil. Add all other ingredients except croutons and lettuce into a jar with a tight lid and shake well. Pour dressing over lettuce that has been washed and thoroughly dried. Add croutons and serve.

Corn Salad

1 – 2 cans whole **corn**, drained, or 2 cups frozen **corn**

chopped **red peppers**

chopped **carrots**

chopped **celery**

chopped **onions**

Dressing

1/4 cup **honey**

1/2 cup **cider vinegar**

garlic powder or crushed **fresh garlic**

salt and **pepper**

1 cup **oil** (omit for dieters)

Mix vegetables together. Mix dressing ingredients and add to salad. This stays for days in refrigerator.

Marinated Eggplant #1

1 large **eggplant**

oil

1 cup **vinegar** mixed with $\frac{1}{2}$ cup **water**

1 cup **ketchup**

3 cloves **garlic**, crushed

$\frac{1}{2}$ tsp. **sugar**

dill

$\frac{1}{2}$ tsp. **hot sauce or** pinch of **chili powder**

Slice eggplant and sprinkle with oil. Bake at 350° until soft (approx. 20 minutes). Mix remaining ingredients together and marinate eggplant. This dish keeps for weeks in the refrigerator.

Marinated Eggplant #2

2 lbs. **eggplant**

$1\frac{1}{2}$ tsp. **salt**

2 **egg whites**

Slice eggplant width-wise $\frac{1}{2}$ " thick. Sprinkle each side with salt. Place on a large tray, overlapping each slice slightly, and allow to drain for 1 – 3 hours.

Do not rinse, but dry with a paper towel.

Whip egg whites with 2 Tbsp. water till frothy. Dip each slice of eggplant in egg whites, scraping off excess on side of bowl. Fry in hot oil till tender and golden. Drain.

Marinade

$\frac{1}{2}$ cup **red wine vinegar**

$\frac{1}{4}$ cup **water**

3 Tbsp. chopped **parsley**

10 cloves **garlic**, crushed

hot chili peppers (optional)

fresh ground pepper

salt to taste

Mix ingredients by hand or in a blender. Layer marinade and eggplants in a container and refrigerate for at least 24 hours. This dish will keep for 7 days in refrigerator.

Serve as a side dish with crackers, or with houmous and techina.

Red Spicy Marinated Eggplant

Follow directions for cooking eggplants in the recipe above, but use this marinade:

¾ cup **ketchup**

½ cup **wine vinegar**

6 cloves **garlic**, pressed

2 Tbsp. chopped fresh **dill**

1 **red hot pepper** (optional)

Marinate exactly as in above recipe.

Roasted Eggplant Relish

2 lbs. **eggplant**

1 cup chopped **onions**

1 clove **garlic**, crushed

¼ cup **oil**

1 Tbsp. fresh **parsley**

2 Tbsp. **mayonnaise**

½ tsp. **salt**

⅛ tsp. **black pepper**

Place washed, unpeeled eggplant directly on the fire of a gas stove, turning occasionally until the skin is charred and blistered all over. Place charred eggplant on a baking tray and bake at 350° for ½ hour. Eggplant will look squashed and shrivelled. Cool.

When eggplant is cool enough to handle, remove pulp from skin and discard skin. Mash pulp with a potato masher or in a food processor.

While eggplant is baking, fry onions and garlic in oil until just beginning to turn brown. Remove from heat and add to eggplant mixture with remaining ingredients. Mix well. Chill. (See next page for hint.)

HINT: Serve with toast, crackers, bread sticks, inside a pita, or with vegetable sticks. It is especially good with lots of chopped raw onions.

Mandarin Orange Salad

1 head **romaine lettuce**

1 **red onion** (yellow or white will do), sliced

11 oz. can **mandarin oranges or** fresh **tangerine** sections

¼ cup chopped **celery**

Dressing

½ cup **sugar**

⅔ cup **oil**

¼ cup **cider vinegar**

1 – 2 Tbsp. **poppy seeds**

1 tsp. **prepared mustard**

Mix together dressing ingredients and toss with salad.

Quick Sweet and Sour Pickles

cucumbers — as many as can fit into the jar of your choosing

24 **peppercorns**

10 **bay leaves**

6 cloves **garlic**

Place cucumbers in jar with peppercorns, bay leaves, and peeled garlic cloves.

Boil together:
1 cup **white vinegar**

3 cups **water**

2 heaped Tbsp. **sugar**

1 Tbsp. **salt**

Pour over cucumbers and let stand for 2-3 hours.

These pickles can be kept for weeks or used within 2-3 hours. Store in refrigerator. When half of pickles are gone, you can add fresh cucumbers.

I always have a jar of pickles in the refrigerator. This is a house special.

Instant Pickles

Pack as many **cucumbers** as you can fit into a jar of 2 quarts or larger.

Fill a quarter of the jar with **vinegar**. Add **water** by cupfuls up to top of the jar, keeping track of how many cups you've used.

Pour liquid from the jar into a pot and bring to a boil.

Now go back to the jar. For each cup of water that you measured, put into the jar 1 Tbsp. **salt** and a generous handful of **peppercorns**, plus 10 or 12 **garlic** cloves, and a large helping of **dill**.

Now pour liquid back into jar and cover tightly.

These delightful pickles can be eaten in hours or days, depending upon how you like your pickles done. Half-sour takes about 24 hours. In the winter I leave them out on the kitchen counter where they get lots of sun.

One of the young men at the Yeshiva, Mark Spiro, loved my pickles. I told him how easy they were to make, and then I left for an extended visit to the States. I came home to find that he didn't miss me so much because he had started making his own pickles. He played with the recipe and came up with a slightly different version of these delightful pickles. I would never admit it, but his are better than mine.

Radish Carrot Salad

4 – 6 large **radishes** or 10 – 12 small

3 large **carrots**

salt and **pepper**

2 Tbsp. **mayonnaise**

¼ cup **vinegar**

pinch of **sugar**

Chop all vegetables in food processor. Season. Add mayonnaise, vinegar, and sugar. Can also be made without mayonnaise. This makes a delightful coleslaw.

Marinated Carrots

2 lbs. **carrots** or enough to fill a glass jar

2 cloves **garlic**

½ tsp. **salt**

¼ cup **oil**

2 Tbsp. **vinegar**

1 tsp. **oregano**

½ tsp. **pepper**

Slice and cook carrots. Mix together rest of ingredients. Place carrots in jar and fill with marinade. Put on tight lid. Turn jar over each day. Best made 1 day ahead. Adjust seasoning.

Marinated Mushrooms

2-4 lbs. **mushrooms**

½ cup **oil**

1 cup **vinegar**

1 **onion**, grated

4 cloves **garlic**

1 – 2 tsp. **sugar**

2 tsp. **salt**

1 **bay leaf**

parsley

Place raw mushrooms in a jar. Mix rest of ingredients and pour over mushrooms. Turn jar every day to marinate evenly. Best made 2 days ahead of serving.

Sesame Noodles

1 lb. fresh **pasta**

1 Tbsp. **salt**

¼ cup **sesame oil**

3 Tbsp. **soy sauce**

¼ tsp. **black pepper**

¼ cup chopped **watercress leaves**

½ cup diced **sweet red peppers**

½ tsp. chopped **garlic**

Boil noodles in 4 quarts water. Drain them straight away and rinse in cold water. Drain well. Put all ingredients in a large bowl and stir immediately. Chill and serve.

Pasta Primavera Salad

4 cups cooked **pasta**

½ cup steamed sliced **zucchini**

½ cup steamed sliced **carrots**

½ cup chopped **green pepper**

½ cup chopped **onions**

2 – 3 **tomatoes**, chopped

1 cup sliced **mushrooms**

4 Tbsp. **mayonnaise**

Parmesan cheese to sprinkle on top (optional)

In a large bowl combine pasta and vegetables. Toss to coat with dressing. Cover and refrigerate for about 30 minutes to allow flavors to blend.

This delightful dish can also be served hot as a main course. Use your creativity! Add or subtract. I add cheese and garlic when I am serving a main dish of Past Primavera.

Potato Salad

5-8 **potatoes**

1 medium-size **onion**, chopped

1 **green or red pepper**, or mixture, chopped

3 stalks **celery**, chopped

mayonnaise to taste, usually 2 or more Tbsp.

salt and **pepper**

½ tsp. **dried mustard or** 1 Tbsp. **prepared mustard**

pickles (optional)

Boil potatoes and peel. Mix all ingredients and taste test for proper seasoning. This is the basic recipe.

There are many variations. Potatoes can be un-peeled—just cut into cubes and follow the same recipe.

Potatoes can be mixed with ½ cup oil (or less) and tons of chopped parsley and dill, along with onions, celery, and green pepper. Season to taste.

Tabbouleh #1

2 cups **bulgur**, soaked and drained

1 cup **olive oil**

1 cup chopped **tomatoes**, canned or fresh

1/8 tsp. **pepper**

1 **onion**, chopped

2 tsp. **mustard**

3/4 tsp. **cumin**

3/4 tsp. **salt**

3/4 tsp. **lemon juice**

1/4 tsp. **sugar**

1/2 tsp. **thyme**

1 tsp. chopped **chives**

2 Tbsp. **parsley**

lots of **garlic**, chopped or crushed

Soak bulgur in boiling water for 20 minutes. Drain and add remaining ingredients. Serve cold.

Tabbouleh #2

1 cup **bulgur**

1 1/2 cups boiling **water**

1 1/2 tsp. **salt**

Soak bulgur in boiling water for 20 minutes with salt, then add:

fresh **black pepper** (to taste)

1/4 cup **lemon juice**

1 heaping tsp. fresh crushed **garlic**

1/4 cup **olive oil**

Refrigerate until well chilled.

Just before serving, add:

1/2 cup chopped **scallions**

1 cup chopped **cucumbers**

1 cup chopped **parsley**

2 medium **tomatoes**, chopped

Three-Bean Salad

½ lb. fresh cooked **yellow beans**

½ lb. fresh cooked **green beans**

½ lb. cooked **chick peas**

1 **green pepper**, chopped

1 **red pepper**, chopped

1 **onion**, chopped or in thinly sliced rings

Dressing

½ cup **oil**

½ cup **vinegar**

½ cup **sugar**

2 tsp. **salt**

½ tsp. **pepper**

1 clove **garlic**, crushed

black olives (optional)

Place all vegetables in a serving bowl. Mix dressing and pour over. This is best made hours before serving.

Bubby Irma's shortcut!

½ pkg. **frozen green beans**

½ pkg. **frozen yellow beans**

1 can **chick peas**

Follow the same directions as above, substituting frozen beans for fresh beans, and as the salad is marinating, the frozen beans thaw. It is a delicious crunchy salad.

SAUCES and DRESSINGS

Barbecue Sauce

7 oz. **ketchup**

salt and **pepper**

1 **onion**, chopped and sautéed

2 small cans **tomato paste**

2 Tbsp. **brown sugar**

2 Tbsp. **vinegar**

2 Tbsp. **grill sauce or steak sauce**

lots and lots of **garlic**, crushed

Mix everything together.

This is a wonderful sauce for all kinds of meat and poultry, and is especially good for outdoor grilling. Marinate the meat or poultry in Barbecue Sauce for about 30 minutes before cooking.

It isn't often that a mother-in-law will admit that her daughter-in-law cooks as well as she does—or even better. This mother-in-law not only admits it, but uses many of her daughter-in-law's recipes. This is one of Elana's specialties.

Belgian Coffee Sauce

1 cup **brown sugar**

1 cup very strong **coffee**

¼ tsp. **vanilla**

1 Tbsp. **brandy**

Boil all ingredients together until thick—10 – 15 minutes. Can be used on ice cream or pancakes.

Easy Curry Sauce

2 – 3 cloves **garlic**

2 – 3 **onions**

1 Tbsp. **curry powder**

1 cup **consommé**

1 Tbsp. **flour**

½ cup **water**

Sauté garlic and onions. Add curry powder and put mixture in a blender or food processor. Add flour, consommé, and water. Blend. Return to fire and heat through.

Can be used over rice or chicken, and is great over steamed vegetables.

Bubby's Special Spaghetti Sauce

3 large **onions**

10 cloves **garlic**

6 lbs. ripe **tomatoes**

salt and **pepper** to taste

½ cup **oregano**

1 Tbsp. **garlic powder**

1 Tbsp. **onion powder**

1 Tbsp. **basil**

1 Tbsp. **soup mix or** 1 cube **vegetable bouillon**

½ tsp. **sugar**

1 large can **tomato puree**

1 can (from puree) **water**

In food processor, chop onions, garlic, and tomatoes, or chop small by hand. Add spices and cook for 1 hour.

Add tomato puree and water, and adjust spices to your taste. Let simmer for 3 – 4 hours. Can be frozen in serving-size portions.

Fast Spaghetti Sauce

1 large **onion**, chopped

1 large clove **garlic**, chopped

1/2 lb. **mushrooms**, fresh or canned

3 – 4 Tbsp. **olive oil**

2 large cans **tomato paste**

1 28 oz. can crushed **tomatoes** or 2 lbs. fresh **tomatoes** crushed in food processor

2 Tbsp. **sugar**

1 tsp. **salt**

1 tsp. **pepper**

1 tsp. **sugar**

2 Tbsp. dried **basil** or 6 large fresh leaves

Fry onion, garlic, and mushrooms in olive oil until brown. Add tomato paste, tomatoes, 3 cups water, and seasoning. Simmer for 1½ hours over low flame.

VARIATION

Meatballs may be added when it begins to simmer. This sauce may also be used for chicken cacciatore, pizza, lasagna, or eggplant Parmesan.

HINT: *Whenever I get the urge to get into serious cooking, I go to the local vegetable store and buy up all the soft tomatoes — at a discount, of course. I usually buy about 10 lbs. at a time. Natie and I wash, blanche, peel, cut, and core them and then pulverize them in the food processor.*

Fresh tomatoes make a difference in any sauce. Used with fresh spices, they give the sauce a gourmet taste. For timesaving, I usually cook all the tomatoes into a spaghetti sauce and freeze in individual serving sizes to be used for spaghetti or any of the dishes mentioned above (see "VARIATION").

Vinaigrette Dressing

1 tsp. finely chopped **onions**

1 Tbsp. **mustard**

3 Tbsp. **wine vinegar**

½ cup **oil**

In a container, combine onions, mustard, vinegar, and oil. Blend well. Cover and store in refrigerator until used.

Creamy Green Dressing

1 cup **mayonnaise**

¼ cup **yogurt or parve cream**

¼ cup chopped **parsley**

1 tsp. chopped **chives**

2 tsp. **vinegar**

¼ tsp. **salt**

dash of **pepper**

Blend all ingredients except mayonnaise in a blender. Fold in mayonnaise. Wonderful on salads.

Vicki's Salad Dressing

1 cup **vinegar**

¼ – ½ cup **sugar**

⅔ cup **ketchup**

2 Tbsp. **mustard**

2 Tbsp. grated **onion**

2 tsp. **salt**

2 tsp. **paprika**

1 or 2 cloves **garlic**

1 cup **oil**

Put all ingredients into blender except oil. Slowly pour oil while blender is running. Keeps in refrigerator for months.

Sweet and Spicy French Dressing

½ cup **sugar**

1 Tbsp. all-purpose **flour**

½ cup **cider vinegar**

1 tsp. **salt**

1 tsp. **Worcestershire sauce**

½ cup finely chopped **onion**

1 clove **garlic**

1 cup **oil**

⅓ cup **ketchup**

1 tsp. **celery seeds**

In a small pan, combine flour, sugar, and vinegar. Cook, stirring, over medium heat until bubbly and thickened. Pour into blender and add salt, Worcestershire sauce, onion, and garlic. Blend until smooth. Set blender on lowest speed and gradually add oil in a slow steady stream. Transfer mixture into a bowl and stir in ketchup and celery seeds. Makes approx. 2 cups. May be stored for 4 weeks in refrigerator.

Toasted Sesame Seed Dressing

2 Tbsp. **sesame seeds**

¼ cup **olive oil or salad oil**

1 Tbsp. **lemon juice**

1 Tbsp. **honey**

1 tsp. **curry powder**

1 cup **sour cream or parve cream**

salt and **pepper**

Spread sesame seeds in a frying pan and cook over medium heat, stirring until golden (3 – 5 minutes). Let cool. In a container, stir together oil, lemon juice, honey, toasted sesame seeds, curry powder, sour cream, salt and pepper. Refrigerate 1 hour to allow flavors to blend. Can be stored up to 5 days. Use on salads or pasta.

Mustard Tarragon Dressing

1 cup **salad oil**

½ cup **tarragon wine vinegar**

¼ cup **Dijon mustard** (if available; otherwise regular mustard)

1 tsp. **salt**

1 tsp. **tarragon leaves**

2 cloves **garlic**

2 hard-boiled **eggs**

Combine all ingredients in a blender and whirl until smooth. Stores well in refrigerator for 1 week. Use on salads.

THE BAAL TESHUVAH

A *baal teshuvah* (one who returns to Judaism) learns many halachos (rules) to follow, along with Jewish Philosophy, Bible History, and Torah instructions for living. When we first became *baalei teshuvah*, I tried very hard to follow all the rules. One Shabbos after dinner, I went into my kitchen to do the dishes, but because I didn't need the dishes for the next meal, Shabbos lunch, I was told that all I should do is stack them neatly and wash them after Shabbos. I did that and put the pots into the oven. After Shabbos, I washed the dishes in the dishwasher.

Two days later, I decided to bake, so I lit the oven and about ten minutes later, I changed my mind and turned it off. The next day I once again prepared to bake, and when I opened the oven to put the cake in, I found my pots — hot and uncleaned. I took them out and what a surprise I got. There was my sterling silver salad set in the big pot. It is a large set with Grand Baroque handles and a heavy black lacquered fork and a spoon on the ends. The fork and spoon had melted completely flat into the shape of abstract faces, but they were still attached to the sterling handles that were now blackened. After a few days, I decided not to send them back to the company to have them replaced. Instead, I put the whole thing on the wall with my other art, and it has become a great conversation piece. I tell everybody that I won first prize in art with this masterpiece, and it is called the *"Baal Teshuvah."*

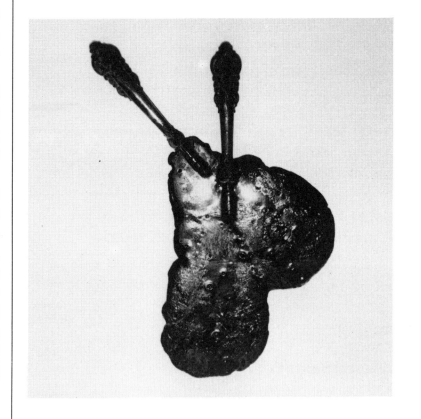

SOUPS and GARNISHES

There is a special knack to making good soup. It is important to taste your soup as it is cooking. If you taste your soup just after you put in the last ingrediant, you will find that it is bland. Soup absorbs flavors as it cooks. Adjust your seasoning as the soup is cooking and then adjust it again just before you are going to serve it. In our house we favor thick soups so we cook it longer. Soup on the second day is even more flavorful. Experiment with your soups and find the perfect one for your family.

Avocado Soup with Chives and Sour Cream

Many people believe that avocado cannot be heated or it will turn bitter. The truth is that it can be heated just to a boil as in this delicious soup, but it should not be cooked longer than that. Be sure the avocados are perfectly ripe.

2 small **avocados**

1 small clove **garlic**

1 cup **parve chicken-flavored soup** made from mix or cube

3¼ cups **milk**

salt and **pepper** to taste

4 Tbsp. **sour cream**

4 tsp. snipped **chives**

Puree avocado flesh in blender with garlic and soup. Add milk, salt, pepper, and sour cream, and blend until smooth and creamy. Sprinkle with chives to serve.

Hot Borscht

2 – 3 **meat bones and/or soup meat**

3 quarts **water**

3 medium or large **beets**, peeled and cubed

½ large head **cabbage**, grated

1 16 oz. can **tomato puree**

½ cup **brown sugar**

salt and **pepper**

Place bones in water and bring them to boil. Skim and reduce heat. Add remaining ingredients. Cover and simmer for 2 – 3 hours.

A wonderful soup that's a meal in itself.

Bubby's Easy Hot Borscht

1 16 oz. can **stewed tomatoes**

1 16 oz. can **red cabbage**

sugar to taste

dill

Given a recipe like this, how can cooking be a chore? Place all ingredients into a pot and heat.

On a chilly night, this is an easy and satisfying appetizer.

Cold Borscht

4 or more large **beets**, peeled and cubed

8 quarts **water**

2 **onions**, chopped

2 Tbsp. **soup mix** (parve or chicken or celery)

garlic powder or fresh garlic to taste

juice of 1 **lemon**

sugar to taste

Place all ingredients in a large pot and cook until beets and onions are tender. Tasting is a very important step, and it is wise to taste it before you refrigerate the borscht. Taste adjustments can be made at any time.

There is one additional step to making a delicious borscht. I take the cooked beets and the cooked onion and put them through the food processor and then back into the borscht. I then add additional fresh onion rings and let them marinate in the borscht.

Serve cold with sour cream and boiled potatoes.

Cream of Spinach Soup

1½ cups **chicken or vegetable stock**

2 pkgs. **frozen spinach**

1 large **onion**, chopped

½ tsp. **nutmeg**

½ tsp. **salt**

¼ tsp. **pepper**

Cook everything together for 7 minutes.

Add:

3 Tbsp. **margarine or butter**

2 cups **parve cream or sour cream**

Pour into blender and add:

2 cans **cream of mushroom soup or** equivalent **mushroom soup powder** plus water.

This is my grandson's favorite meal. It is served at least once a week in Debi's house.

Chicken Soup

chicken pieces from as many chickens as you are using for your dinner, or one whole chicken.

3 quarts water

4 – 5 carrots

3 stalks celery

2 medium to large onions

2 heaping Tbsp. chicken soup mix

fresh parsley

fresh dill

salt and pepper (I use very little salt in chicken soup, because the chickens have been salted in the kashering and the soup mix is also salted. I do add pepper to taste.)

garlic, fresh or powder

As I am cleaning my chickens and cutting them into serving-size pieces, I put aside the necks, wings, backs, and small pieces of skin. This is what I use for my chicken soup. There are many tricks and secrets for making chicken soup, and I hesitate giving my secrets away; however, I don't think I have a choice.

Boil chicken parts in a large pot that is ¾ full with water. Chicken pieces give off what my mother called scum. It is important to remove the scum so that you will have a clear soup. When this is done, add carrots, celery stalks, and onions. Cook this on medium heat for ½ hour. Add chicken soup mix. Let cook for 1 hour on a low flame.

The Trick: *When the soup is almost finished cooking, throw in a large handful of fresh parsley and dill. Adding these herbs near the end makes all the difference. The soup retains that fresh flavor and aroma.*

Hint: *To make a truly golden soup, add two or three pieces of onion skin.*

In our house, it is foolish to make a small pot of chicken soup. I love having my freezer stocked with soup. Every once in a while I get a call from a young man with a raspy throat asking if I possibly have some leftover soup to help cure his cold. I pop the soup in the microwave and have it piping hot when he comes to the door. A little of Bubby's Chicken Soup served in a home away from home does wonders.

Often when I am in a hurry on Friday, I defrost a frozen container of soup and use it as a base, just adding more ingredients if necessary. It can be used as a base for vegetable soup, bean and barley soup, or any other soups that require a stock.

Hot and Sour Soup

Hot and Sour Soup for my Chinese dinners is always made with leftover **chicken soup,** adding **vinegar, soy sauce,** and a few drops of **hot sauce.** For that extra special gourmet touch, I add fresh **bean sprouts** and crispy **cabbage.**

Curry Vegetable Chowder

1 medium **onion**, chopped

¼ lb. **mushrooms**, chopped

1 **green pepper**, chopped

1 large stalk **celery**, chopped

2 large **potatoes**, cooked and cubed

1 large or 2 small **carrots**, chopped

2 quarts **water**

1 cup **milk or parve cream**

1 Tbsp. **miso** (soybean paste, available in health food stores) — optional.

salt, **pepper**, and **curry powder** to taste, plus your favorite spices.

Sauté onion, mushrooms, pepper, and celery until transparent. Boil water, milk, and miso, and add vegetables. Season to taste and cook until all vegetables are tender.

Curried Lentil Soup

1 cup **lentils**

6 cups **water**

1 heaping Tbsp. **chicken soup powder**

2 medium **onions**, chopped

2 cloves **garlic**, chopped

2 medium **potatoes**, thinly sliced

curry spices: 1 tsp. more or less, of each

    curry powder

    coriander

    ginger

    cumin

$1/2$ tsp. **chili powder**

1 can crushed or 4 fresh chopped **tomatoes**

additional **garlic or garlic powder** to taste

juice of 1 **lemon**

Boil lentils in water until they are soft. Add potatoes and continue to cook.

In a second soup pot, sauté onions and garlic. Add spices. Add some of the lentil broth and water — as much as 3 cups can be added — to the sauté. The spices begin to make a thick paste. Continue to sauté and add a bit more broth if needed. Transfer into soup, and add soup powder. If you like a thicker soup, you can add a heaping tablespoon of mushroom soup mix. Add tomatoes, extra garlic, and lemon juice.

This richly flavored soup was discovered in Nairobi. Vicki, my gourmet critic, experimented with all the spices of Africa and became an authority on the flavors of these unusual spices.

This is a delightful winter soup. It warms you instantly. I serve it with sour cream or yogurt for a milchig dinner, or without if you want it parve.

Minestrone Soup

1 **onion**, chopped

1 **leek** (optional), chopped

1 – 2 cloves **garlic**, chopped

chopped **parsley**

chopped **basil**

3 – 5 quarts **water**

½ lb. dry **white beans**, soaked in water overnight

1 tsp. **olive oil**

1 small can **tomato paste**

2 – 3 fresh **tomatoes**, pureed in blender or food processor

3 – 4 **celery stalks**

2 – 3 **carrots**

2 – 3 **potatoes**

1 cup **chick peas**, cooked or canned

1 **turnip**

¼ **cabbage**, shredded

2 – 3 **zucchinis**, chopped

1 cup **elbow macaroni**

salt to taste

½ tsp. **black pepper**

Sauté onion, leek, garlic, parsley, and basil in oil until transparent. Do not burn!!! In a large soup pot filled with water, add vegetables and sautéed onion mixture. Cook on high flame until boiling, then lower flame and simmer for 2 – 3 hours.

Serve with grated Parmesan cheese.

Hint: A fast way of cooking beans: Boil beans in water for 2 minutes. Remove from heat and cover for one hour. Then cook them with the soup.

Gazpacho (Spicy Cold Tomato Soup)

3 cloves **garlic**

1 **onion**

2 **cucumbers**

2 fresh **tomatoes**

1 **green pepper**

½ tsp. **salt**

⅛ tsp. **cayenne pepper**

¼ cup **vinegar**

¼ cup **olive oil**

¾ cup **tomato juice**

Mix all ingredients and chop together in a blender or food processor. Adjust seasoning to taste.

Serve cold for a zesty summer soup.

Hint: *Leftover salads make a great base for Gazpacho.*

Leek Soup

1½ lbs. **potatoes**

6 cups **water**

2 Tbsp. **butter**

3 **leeks**, chopped

1 **onion**, chopped

garlic to taste, chopped

1 Tbsp. **salt**

1 **egg yolk**

1 cup **milk**

2 Tbsp. **soup mix or soup stock**

Boil potatoes in water until tender. Add other ingredients and cook for ½ hour. If soup needs to be thickened, use 2 Tbsp. flour mixed into a paste with water. Serve with croutons.

Mushroom, Garlic, and Barley Soup

1 **onion**, chopped

3 cloves **garlic**, chopped

1 lb. **mushrooms**, sliced

1 cup **barley**, cooked according to package directions

1½ quarts **soup stock** or 1½ quarts water boiled with 1 heaping Tbsp. any soup mix plus 1 heaping Tbsp. mushroom soup mix

3 Tbsp. **soy sauce**

3 – 4 Tbsp. **dry white wine**

salt and **pepper** to taste

Sauté onion with garlic and mushrooms. Add barley to boiling soup stock, and then add mushroom mixture.

Add seasonings and allow to boil for 30 – 40 minutes. Serve with garlic bread or croutons.

During the Gulf War I had some young students staying at our house. I really couldn't figure out if they just wanted to be in a family atmosphere or they were worried about us being alone. Whatever, we stayed a close-knit family until the war was over. I tried making interesting meals, and one day decided to make this recipe that was given to me along time ago. I made it and they all loved it. Two weeks later, I wanted to make it again, so I read the recipe over to be sure I had all the ingredients in the house, and proceeded to make the soup. At one point, I reread the recipe and burst out laughing. When I read the entire recipe with all the instructions, I found that I had made a delicious soup out of what was supposed to be a mushroom, garlic, and barley casserole. That's a Bubby Irma story.

Fruit soup is one of the summer recipes that can always be found in my freezer or refrigerator. It is the most refreshing summer soup.

However, it is difficult to give you an exact recipe. So, come into my refrigerator with me and we'll see what we find. First, take all the soft fruits and put them on the table. Then, pick what is usable and begin washing and cutting up the fruit. Discard all pits, and peel any that need peeling. I usually peel everything. Fill a pot with water and begin cooking the fruit. For seasoning, I use lemonade or lemon juice and sugar — and have on occasion used iced tea mix. We love cinnamon, and I use it every chance I can. If I have cinnamon sticks, I also use them — 1 or 2 sticks. I never make a small pot of anything — so I use at least an 8-quart pot and keep a supply in the refrigerator all summer. I have frozen it for picnics or long trips and it is great.

In the U.S.A. you can get frozen blueberries and raspberries — what a treat!! Use them and enjoy a rare delicacy.

Fruit Soup #1

All **summer fruits**: peaches, plums, apples, pears, etc.

cinnamon and/or cinnamon sticks to taste

Peel and pit fruit and cut into bite-size pieces.

I find that 10 lbs. makes an 8-quart pot of soup. Fill pot with water and add fruit. Boil for 15 minutes until all the fruit is soft. Add cinnamon and/or cinnamon sticks. Add sugar if necessary — I sometimes use sugar substitute. Allow soup to cool, and refrigerate for several hours before serving.

Fruit Soup # 2

Blend all the prepared **fruit** in a blender. Add **cinnamon** and a healthy portion of **white wine**. Chill before serving.

This delicious fruit soup wins the prize for getting the most compliments.

Farina Dumplings

1 **egg**, beaten well

½ cup, more or less, **semolina**

1 Tbsp. chopped **parsley**

salt and **pepper**

Add semolina to egg, beating with a fork until it is smooth and thick but runny. Add parsley.

Refrigerate for 20 minutes only — it will stiffen. Add salt and peeper and drop by teaspoons into boiling soup.

These delightful light dumplings can be used in any soup and are especially good in chicken soup and cholent. They also freeze very well.

Matzah Balls (Kneidlach)

3 **eggs**

5 Tbsp. **chicken fat**

½ cup **water**

1 cup **matzah meal**

1 tsp. **salt**

Beat eggs well until they are light and frothy. Add rest of ingredients and beat until thick. Set aside for ½ hour. Form balls and drop them into boiling soup. May also be boiled separately in boiling water and then added to soup.

Feather-Weight Matzah Balls

4 **eggs**

⅓ cup melted **shortening or oil**

½ cup **soda water** (seltzer)

1 tsp. **salt**

pepper to taste

1 cup **matzah meal**

Beat eggs well and add shortening, soda water, salt, and pepper. Beat thoroughly. Slowly add matzah meal. Refrigerate for 20 minutes. Form matzah balls using wet hands, and drop into 1½ quarts boiling water that has an additional teaspoon of salt added, or into boiling soup.

Croutons

Can be bought in the supermarkets, but can also be made at home. Cut **bread** into small squares and flavor them with **garlic powder**. Bake in a hot oven until croutons are toasted, but be careful not to burn them.

VEGETABLES

Cauliflower — Marsala Gobhi

2 lbs. **cauliflower**

⅓ cup **oil**

3 large **tomatoes**, quartered

3 large **onions**, grated

5 cloves **garlic**

2 tsp. grated **ginger**

⅓ cup **water**

⅛ tsp. **chili powder**

1 tsp. **coriander**

1 tsp. **cumin**

salt and **pepper** to taste

1 lb. small **potatoes** (or sliced large potatoes), boiled

¼ lb. **peas**

1 Tbsp. **cream or parve cream**

½ tsp. **sugar**

Fry cauliflower in oil — a few pieces at a time until golden brown. Drain on paper towels. Crush tomatoes in processor or chop very fine.

Heat a bit more oil and add onions. Sauté until lightly colored. Grind garlic and ginger, and make a paste with the water. Add to onions, stirring.

Add chili, coriander, cumin, salt, and pepper into onions and continue to cook for 1 minute. Add cauliflower, potatoes, peas, and tomatoes.

Cook for 5 minutes, then stir in cream and sugar.

When I see a recipe with so many ingredients I usually shy away from it, thinking that it's not worth the effort. However, this one is. Try it!!!

Potato Casserole

Slice **potatoes** very thin — amount to be determined by number of guests. Layer potatoes in a casserole with lots of fresh, crushed **garlic**, grated **cheese**, **salt, pepper,** and a little **butter.** Cover with **milk.** Bake until potatoes are cooked. Yummm!!!

A typical Kenyan dish that has won the hearts of all garlic lovers. When Vicki comes from Kenya, it is one of the first dishes she makes for her father.

French-cut String Bean Casserole

2 15½ oz. cans **French-cut string beans**

2 oz. **almonds**, chopped or whole

1 can **cream of mushroom soup or powdered mushroom soup** made with **parve cream or milk**, keeping it a bit thicker than usual

1 cup **breadcrumbs**

2 oz. **margarine**, melted

Place first 3 ingredients into a casserole. Top with breadcrumbs and melted margarine. Bake at 350° for 30 minutes.

Ratatouille

1 **onion**, chopped

4 cloves **garlic**, chopped

4 Tbsp. **olive oil**

1 cup cubed **eggplant**

1 **green pepper**, diced

1 **red pepper**, diced

1 **potato**, diced

1 **tomato**, diced

¼ lb. **mushrooms**, fresh or canned

1 tsp. **oregano**

1 tsp. **zatar** (a combination of Middle Eastern spices found in Israel) — optional

Sauté onion and garlic in oil until translucent. Add vegetables (not mushrooms) and let simmer until they are all cooked — but not overdone. Add mushrooms and simmer for another 2 minutes. Salt and pepper to taste.

Spinach Squares

2 pkgs. **frozen chopped spinach**

3 Tbsp. **butter**

1 small **onion**, grated

¼ lb. **mushrooms**, sliced

4 **eggs**

¼ cup fine dry **breadcrumbs**

1 can **cream of mushroom soup or** equivalent made with **dried mushroom soup** and **water**

⅛ tsp. **pepper**

⅛ tsp. **oregano**

⅛ tsp. **basil**

Mix everything together. Bake in a 9" square pan at 350° for 35 minutes. Cut into squares and serve hot or cold.

Sweet Potato Pie

2 lbs. **sweet potatoes**, cooked and mashed

1 Tbsp. **butter or margarine**

½ tsp. **cinnamon**

¾ tsp. **salt**

1 – 2 Tbsp. **honey**

nuts (optional)

1 unbaked **piecrust**

Mix all ingredients in a bowl and put them into piecrust. Bake at 350° for 45 minutes.

VARIATION

I put sliced pineapple or canned apricots or peaches on top of the pie. Last week I made this sweet potato delight without the piecrust — I scooped the sweet potatoes into peach halves and baked them in a casserole. They were very special.

Shakshouka

4 Tbsp. **oil**

1 large **onion**, chopped

3 ripe **tomatoes**, chopped

1 red **pepper**, diced

2 cloves **garlic**, crushed

1 cup **water**

1 small can **tomato paste**

6 **eggs**

Heat oil and sauté vegetables. Add water and tomato paste and bring to boil. Crack each egg into a glass, then drop into vegetables and cover them with sauce. Poach for 5 – 10 minutes on medium heat. Salt and pepper to taste.

Shakshouka Bubby Style

One evening I had a strong craving for shakshouka. I looked all over for a recipe and couldn't find one that fit with the ingredients that I had in the house. So, I took stock of my cupboard and found:

½ large can **tomato paste**

¼ cup **harissa** (crushed red peppers and tomatoes — hot)

1 – 2 cups **water**

6 **eggs**

I mixed the first 3 ingredients, brought them to a boil, and dropped whole eggs into the boiling sauce.

It was fabulous. One of the best dishes I have ever made. Natie is still talking about it.

Tomato Pie

2 lbs. **tomatoes**

3 **onions**

2 cloves **garlic**, crushed

2 Tbsp. **flour**

1 tsp. **salt**

½ tsp. **pepper**

1 cup **parve cream**

1 Tbsp. **celery soup mix**

1 Tbsp. **mushroom soup mix**

2 Tbsp. **tomato paste**

1 tsp. **basil**

pinch of **thyme**

2 **egg whites**

oil for frying

1 **pie shell**, partially cooked

Process fresh tomatoes in food processor or blender. Slice onions and sauté them. Add tomatoes and continue to cook until it becomes slightly thick. When mixture cools down, it becomes thicker. Add rest of ingredients and bake in pie shell at 350° for 30 – 40 minutes.

Tomato Pie Bubby Style

1 **piecrust**, unbaked

1 quart container **Bubby's Spaghetti Sauce** from freezer

2 **egg whites**

Add egg whites to spaghetti sauce, and adjust seasoning if needed. Pour into crust. Bake at 350° for 30 – 40 minutes. Serve hot, but may also be eaten cold.

Vegetable Quiche

1 lb. **broccoli or any** combination of **vegetables** (frozen or fresh) e.g., zucchini or mixed vegetables

3 **eggs**

3 Tbsp. **mayonnaise**

½ cup **water**

2½ Tbsp. **onion soup mix**

1 – 2 Tbsp. **flour**

Place vegetables in casserole or baking dish. Combine remaining ingredients and pour mixture over vegetables. Bake at 350° for 30 – 40 minutes until brown on top.

Zucchini

Cut 4 – 6 **zucchinis** in half, length-wise. Steam them in a microwave, or in a couscous pot, or even a regular pot. Serve immediately with **salt** and **butter or margarine**.

The delicate flavor of this simple dish is a delightful surprise. It tastes just like corn on the cob.

I often use this when I feel that the dinner is heavy and a steamed vegetable is the order of the day.

POULTRY and MEAT

Chinese Pancakes with Moo Shu Beef or Chicken

Filling

1½ lbs. lean **meat or chicken**

4 **green onions**, cut into 2" pieces

1 Tbsp. **cornstarch**

½ tsp. **sugar**

¼ cup **soy sauce**

2 Tbsp. **sherry or white wine**

3 **eggs**, lightly beaten

½ cup **oil**

½ lb. **mushrooms**, sliced

bamboo shoots, cut into strips (if available)

¼ head **cabbage**, shredded

1 tsp. **salt**

½ lb. fresh **bean sprouts**

1 tsp. **garlic powder**

1 tsp. **ground ginger**

Cut meat into thin strips, matchstick size. If I use chicken, I often buy boned white chicken meat.

Combine meat, onions, cornstarch, sugar, soy sauce, and wine. Set aside to marinate at least ½ hour.

Scramble eggs in a little oil, stirring constantly so they break up into pea-size pieces. Set aside in a bowl.

In the same frying pan, heat ¼ cup oil until very hot. Stir-fry mushrooms, bamboo shoots, cabbage, and salt. Cook until vegetables are tender-crisp. Set aside.

Heat ¼ cup more oil until very hot. Add meat mixture and stir-fry for about 3 minutes. Add eggs and bean sprouts last. Stir-fry until heated through. Add more cornstarch if a thicker consistency is desired.

This wonderful Chinese dish can also be made with just vegetables for the vegetarians in the crowd.

Pancakes

2½ cups **flour**

½ tsp. **salt**

1 cup **boiling water**

2 tsp. **vegetable oil**

Combine flour and salt, and gradually add boiling water, blending with a fork until mixture forms pea-sized balls. Press into a ball and knead — dough will be stiff. Shape dough into a long roll, about 16". Cut roll into 16 pieces. Cover pieces with a damp cloth.

Lay 2 pieces on a lightly floured board and flatten them out with your hand. Brush oil on top of each piece and place pieces together top-to-top. Roll out the two pancakes together into a circle 7" – 8". Use all 16 pieces and stack them until ready to cook.

In an ungreased skillet on medium heat, cook pancakes until light brown spots appear. Turn pancakes and cook second side until light brown spots appear.

Remove from skillet and *immediately* separate the halves, making two thin pancakes. Stack them on a plate (browned side up) and cover with a damp cloth.

Pancakes can be made ahead of time and frozen. To heat them, I put the entire batch into the microwave and defrost them for about 2 minutes. The pancakes are best served warm. If frozen or chilled in the refrigerator, they can be heated through in the stack in a 350° oven for 10 – 15 minutes.

TO SERVE:
Pass the pancakes and let each person spread a small amount of hot Chinese Mustard and Sweet and Sour Sauce on the pancake. Then place about 1/4 cup meat or chicken mixture onto center of pancake and fold to form an envelope-style roll to be eaten with your fingers.

I am always amazed at the response to this delicious dish. Conversation flows freely as each person struggles to get the pancake filled. It is one of my favorite dishes and can be easily adapted to whatever you have in the refrigerator.

Chinese Mustard

Spoon out 1 Tbsp. **mustard powder** into a small dish. Make into a paste with **water** until it reaches desired consistency. Serve with all your Chinese dinners.

Sweet and Sour Sauce

There are many ways to make this sauce. One day I didn't have all the ingredients so I improvised. I took a jar of preserves (jam) out of the fridge and put in some Chinese Mustard and garlic powder. It was an instant success.

1/2 cup **vinegar**

1 cup **water or juice from canned pineapple**

1 tsp. **chicken soup powder**

3/4 cup **sugar** (only 1/2 cup if juice is used. Sugar may be brown or white.)

1 tsp. **lemon juice**

1 Tbsp. **cornstarch**

2 Tbsp. **water**

2 Tbsp. **soy sauce**

In a small pot combine first 5 ingredients. Dissolve cornstarch in 2 Tbsp. water and add soy sauce. Stir into sauce and boil until it becomes clear and thick.

VARIATION

Add cup-up green pepper, pickles, and fruit. I often make this a bit thicker and use it for duck sauce with a Chinese dinner.

Crispy Chinese Chicken Pieces

4 **chicken breasts**

2 Tbsp. **soy sauce**

1 tsp. **oil**

1 tsp. **salt**

1 tsp. **gin or cognac**

cornstarch

Cut chicken into bite-size pieces and marinate in soy sauce, oil, salt, and gin for ½ hour. Dip chicken pieces into cornstarch and fry till crisp.

Serve with Sweet and Sour Sauce (see above recipe) plus boiled rice.

Chicken and Almonds

2 lbs. **chicken breasts**, boned

2 Tbsp. **oil**

½ cup **white wine**

½ tsp. **ground ginger**

1 tsp. **garlic powder**

1 Tbsp. **cornstarch**

2 Tbsp. **soy sauce**

4 oz. **almonds**, whole or chopped

Cut chicken breasts into thin (2") strips.

Mix rest of ingredients except for almonds, and marinate chicken for 1 hour or more. Stir-fry until cooked and add almonds. Serve over rice.

A Chinese dinner is always a treat for us. Hot and Sour Soup made from leftover Shabbos Chicken Soup, Moo Shu Pancakes filled with chicken and vegetables, plus marinated stir-fried Chicken and Almonds always satisfies our yen for Chinese culinary delights.

Chicken and Wine

1 heaping Tbsp. **mushroom soup mix**

1 heaping Tbsp. **chicken soup mix**

1 cup **parve cream**

4 cups **water**

1 **green** and **1 red pepper**, chopped

$1/4$ lb. **mushrooms**, fresh or canned

1 or 2 **chickens**, cut into serving pieces

garlic powder

1 cup **dry white wine**

Place first 6 ingredients into a large kettle and simmer. Toss chicken pieces in garlic powder and place into kettle. Cook on medium flame for $1 1/2$ hours. Chicken should be done — but not too soft.

Seasoning can be adjusted to taste. Adding wine at last stages of cooking helps to retain its flavor. I often have to thicken the gravy with flour or cornstarch after wine is added.

Serve over rice and be sure to make enough for leftovers.

VARIATION

A few weeks ago I had to make a fancy dinner in a hurry. The chickens in the freezer were gone, and I didn't have time to go and get more. I got a chance to practice what I preach — use the ingredients you have in the house!!

I found turkey schnitzel (boneless turkey breasts) in the freezer and quickly defrosted them in the microwave. I sautéed onions and mushrooms and put them into a bowl with breadcrumbs to form a stuffing — adding water and seasoning: garlic, salt, and pepper. I then flattened the turkey breasts by pounding them on a board — you can use a meat pounder or do it the easy way as I do: flatten them out with your hand. I spread the stuffing over the turkey and rolled it up like a jelly roll, then I placed each roll carefully into the same sauce as for Chicken and Wine. It was super!

Chicken and Yams

4 large **yams**, peeled and sliced thin

1 **onion**, sliced

1 **chicken**, cut up

garlic powder

¼ cup **chopped walnuts**

2 oz. **margarine**, melted

¼ cup **prepared mustard**

¼ cup **honey**

¼ cup **orange juice**

Arrange yams and onion on bottom of a baking pan. Place chicken on top and sprinkle with garlic powder. Combine nuts with rest of ingredients and pour mixture over chicken and yams. Cover with tin foil and bake at 375° for 1 hour, basting every 15 minutes. When chicken is tender, uncover and bake until browned.

The success of this chicken depends largely on the sweetness of the yams.

Garlic, Dill, and Lemon Chicken

2 **chickens**, cut into pieces

3 – 4 cloves **garlic** or garlic granules

1 cup **white wine**

fresh **dill**

lemon juice, fresh or bottled

fresh **mushrooms**

2 **oranges**

Rub chicken with garlic.

Lay chicken in baking dish and pour white wine over it. Cut fresh dill into small pieces and sprinkle over chicken. Squeeze lemon juice on top.

Allow chicken to marinate ½ hour or longer.

When you are ready to bake chicken, add more wine and mushrooms. Bake for 1½ hours, basting often. Cut large slices of orange and add to chicken for last 20 minutes of baking.

Hawaiian Chicken

1 or 2 **chickens**, cut into serving-size pieces

garlic powder

Sprinkle chicken with garlic powder and brown in a 400° oven for 40 minutes.

Sauce

1 cup **brown sugar**

2 Tbsp. **cornstarch**

1/3 cup **vinegar**

1 cup **pineapple juice**

1/2 tsp. **salt**

2 Tbsp. **soy sauce**

onions

green and **red peppers**, sliced

1 20 oz. **can pineapple slices**

Combine sugar, cornstarch, vinegar, juice, salt, and soy sauce in a pan, and cook until thick and clear.

Layer onions, peppers, and pineapple over browned chicken and spoon sauce over all. Bake at 350° for 1 hour.

I bake this in a rectangular pyrex casserole dish that fits into a silver server. The green and red peppers plus the pineapple rings make this a beautiful presentation.

Crispy Garlic Chicken

chickens, cut into serving-size pieces that have been rubbed with **fresh garlic** and **sweet paprika**.

salt and **pepper** to taste. Kosher chickens generally do not need salt, but pepper brings out the flavors.

Roast in an open roasting pan, placing tin foil on chicken for first 45 minutes. Uncover for 45 minutes more or until browned and crisp. If lots of gravy is desired, then add water to bottom of pan while it is cooking.

Mocha Garlic Chicken

2 **chickens**, cut into pieces

garlic powder

$1/4$ tsp. **cocoa**

1 cup **coffee** made with 1 heaping Tbsp. **instant coffee**

$1/3$ cup **ketchup**

3 Tbsp. **soy sauce**

2 Tbsp. fresh **lemon juice**

2 Tbsp. **wine vinegar or plain vinegar plus** 1 Tbsp. **wine**

$1/3$ cup **brown sugar**

2 Tbsp. **cornstarch**

Dust chicken pieces with garlic powder and place in a pan — I prefer to use a cooking bag.

Mix all other ingredients in a pot and bring to a boil. Pour this sauce over chicken pieces. Bake for 1 – 2 hours.

Baking this in a bag gives the best gravy. It comes out browned and flavorful. Use over rice or mashed potatoes with steamed carrot sticks. ---- it looks beautiful. Natie has it over slices of challah.

Brisket

4 – 6 lb. **brisket**

3 Tbsp. **onion soup**

garlic powder

Place brisket on a large piece of tin foil or in a cooking bag with onion soup and garlic powder. Wrap tightly and bake for 2-3 hours. Gravy will form, and you can add peeled potatoes and carrots and cook them in the same wrapping.

It is best to let brisket cool and dhen slice it very thin. The gravy will be rich and plentiful.

Chili con Carne

1 cup **beans (white or red)**

chilies (small, but hot) to your taste

2 **onions**, chopped

2 lbs. **ground beef or soya substitute**

1 Tbsp. **olive oil**

2 **bay leaves**

1 Tbsp. **cumin**

2 cloves **garlic**, chopped

oregano to taste

2 Tbsp. **paprika**

1 tsp. **sugar**

salt and **pepper** to taste

It is advisable to soak beans overnight. Soak chilies in boiling water for 30 minutes. Drain, reserving liquid in case mixture becomes too thick. Brown onions and meat in oil. Add rest of ingredients and cook for 2 hours on low flame. Stir often so that beans do not stick to the bottom. This can be used as a Shabbos cholent!

Hint: *If you use red beans, soak overnight and cook for 1 hour before adding to Chili.*

If you are in a hurry, as I usually am, I have come up with a fast and delicious recipe.

Bubby's Simple Chili #1

1 quart container **Bubby's Spaghetti Sauce**, defrosted

1 16 oz. can **baked beans**

chili powder

lots of **garlic**, fresh or powdered

1 tsp. **cumin**

Add baked beans to spaghetti sauce. Sprinkle in spices. Heat together and serve with crisp crackers and chopped fresh onions.

Bubby's Simple Chili #2

Leftover **Cholent #1** (see below) with **chili powder, cumin,** and **tomato paste** added.

Cholent #1

3 **onions**, chopped

3 cloves **garlic**, chopped

1 lb. **beef cubes**

2 **carrots**, chopped

1 **sweet potato**, cubed

½ cup **barley**

5 – 6 **potatoes**, cubed

½ cup **white beans**

½ cup **red beans**

2 Tbsp. **soy sauce**

salt and **pepper** to taste

water to cover all the ingredients

Brown onions, garlic, and meat. Add rest of ingredients, and allow to boil rapidly for ½ hour. Lower heat and let simmer for 1 hour. Before *blech* is put on for Shabbos, add more boiled water to pot.

Cholent #2

3 **onions**

1 **zucchini**

4 **carrots**

1 **sweet potato**

5 **white potatoes**

½ cup **rice**

½ cup **barley**

½ cup **kasha**

2 Tbsp. **soy sauce**

salt, pepper, and **garlic**

meat (optional) **or chicken** (optional)

Chop vegetables.

Place all ingredients in a pot with water to cover and cook for ½ hour, then lower flame and allow to simmer for another hour. Place on *blech*, making sure the water is covering all the ingredients. Place kishke (see below) on top.

Kishke for Cholent

12 oz. **onion crackers**

2 **carrots**

2 stalks **celery**

1 **onion**

4 oz. **margarine**, melted

1 **egg**

salt, pepper, and **garlic** to taste

Mix all ingredients in food processor and form into logs — should make 2 or 3 rolls. Roll in tin foil. Bake at 375° for approx. 1 hour or until solid. Warm on top of a pot on *blech* and serve with cholent.

I prefer to cook the kishke right in the cholent, wrapped in the tin foil. Kept on the *blech* all night, it absorbs the flavor and juices of the cholent.

Without meat in the cholent, this recipe is easily adapted for vegetarians. Just alter the seasoning.

Cholent with Meat

1 – 1½ lbs. **flanken** with **bones**

1 medium **onion**, sliced

1 clove **garlic**, chopped

½ cup **barley**

3 medium **potatoes**, cubed

1 cup mixed **kidney and lima beans**

1 **bay leaf**

salt and **pepper** to taste

Soak beans for 24 hours in boiling water, changing water 2 or 3 times.

In a deep pot, brown flanken and bones, onions, and garlic. When these have browned, add barley, potatoes, and beans. Add water to cover. Add bay leaf, salt, and pepper, and cook for 1 hour. Before placing cholent on *blech*, cook in 3 Tbsp. bottled or homemade barbecue sauce. Cover and leave on *blech* overnight.

PARVE CHOLENT

Use above recipe, omitting meat and adding 2-3 Tbsp. oil to fry onions and 1 Tbsp. for additional seasoning.

Stuffed Steak

10 slices **shoulder steak**, cut very thin

garlic powder or granules

Ask your butcher to slice the steak tissue-paper thin. And even then, when you go to prepare it, pound it flat with the heel of your hand. Sprinkle each piece liberally with garlic powder or granules.

Stuffing

1 **onion**

1 Tbsp. **oil**

1½ cups **breadcrumbs**

salt and **pepper** to taste

¼ cup **water**

Chop onion and sauté in oil until translucent. Add breadcrumbs, salt, pepper, and water. Place a thin layer of stuffing onto each piece of steak and roll it up like a jelly roll. Don't use a toothpick to secure it — it may not be visible, and cause problems for the person eating it. If you need the security of closing the roll, use white sewing thread and wind it around the roll. Otherwise, just handle it carefully and drop it into the sauce.

Sauce

1 **onion**

fresh mushrooms (optional)

1 **green pepper**

1 clove fresh **garlic**, crushed

1 Tbsp. **oil**

1 small can **tomato paste**

1 28 oz. can **crushed tomatoes**

Sauté onion, mushrooms, green pepper, and garlic in oil. Add tomato paste and crushed tomatoes, then place the steak rolls into the bubbling sauce — carefully. Cook for 1 hour on a medium flame until steak is tender.

This recipe is one of the most unusual and delicious meat dishes. It was my mother's creation. The quantities will vary with the amount of guests you are feeding. I usually make this for a crowd of eight.

FISH and DAIRY DISHES

Flounder or Sole Fillets with Grapes

½ lb. **mushrooms**, sliced

3 Tbsp. **butter**

salt and **pepper**

2 lbs. **flounder or sole fillets**

1 cup **milk**

4 Tbsp. **butter**

1½ Tbsp. **flour**

2 Tbsp. **Parmesan cheese**, grated

½ cup **light cream or milk**

½ lb. **seedless grapes**

extra grated **cheese**

½ cup **white wine** (optional)

Sauté mushrooms in 3 Tbsp. butter, and season with salt and pepper. Simmer fish in milk for 5 – 10 minutes. Remove fish carefully from pot, using a slotted spoon, and keep the liquid. In another pot, melt 4 Tbsp. butter. Remove from fire and add flour. Slowly add milk from fish. Add cheese and cream. Return to fire and stir until it thickens.

Arrange fish, mushrooms, and grapes in a buttered casserole. Cover with sauce and heat. Add more cheese and wine if desired, and bake at 400° for 15 minutes.

Tuna Casserole

1 16 oz. pkg. **noodles**, cooked

3 Tbsp. **mushroom soup mix** plus ½ cup **water or** 1 can **condensed mushroom soup**

1-2 cans **tuna**

½ cup **mayonnaise**

½ cup chopped **onions**

½ cup chopped **celery**

4 slices **cheese** — your favorite

½ cup **milk**

Drain noodles thoroughly and mix in next 5 ingredients. Put into a greased casserole. Melt cheese in milk and pour over casserole. Bake at 350° until a crust forms on top.

Spaghetti with Salmon

1 16 oz. pkg. **spaghetti or** any preferred **pasta**

1¼ cups **cream** (use low-fat milk for the dieters)

2 Tbsp. **flour**

¼ lb. sliced **smoked salmon or 1 can salmon**

garlic salt to taste

pepper to taste

¼ cup **white wine**

chopped **chives** for garnish

Boil spaghetti in salted water. Heat cream and add flour. Mix in salmon and season to taste. Pour cream and salmon over noodles and mix. Garnish with chopped chives.

Hot Seafood Casserole

3 medium **green peppers**, diced

14 oz. can **mushrooms**

¼ cup **oil**

1½ lbs. **haddock or any other fish**, cooked 15 minutes and flaked

2 hard-boiled **eggs**

1 Tbsp. **prepared mustard**

1½ cups **mayonnaise**

1½ tsp. **salt**

1 raw **egg**

pinch **cayenne pepper**

paprika

Sauté peppers and mushrooms in oil for 15 minutes. Add fish, hard-boiled eggs, mustard, and 1 cup mayonnaise.

Add in salt, raw egg, and cayenne pepper. Mix everything and put into a baking dish. Spread remaining mayonnaise on top and sprinkle with paprika. Bake for 20 minutes or until brown.

Nile Perch

1 large piece **Nile perch**

juice of 1 fresh **lemon**

A must: Soak fish steak in lemon juice for 1 hour as it is defrosting. Rinse fish lightly and place on a piece of tin foil large enough to wrap around it.

Sauce

½ cup **mayonnaise**

1 tsp. **dried mustard**

¼ cup **ketchup**

½ cup **sour cream**

Mix sauce ingredients and spread over fish. Wrap tightly in tin foil and bake for 30 minutes or until fish meat appears white when pricked with a fork. Can be served hot or cold.

Nile perch can also be ground and made into delicious white gefilte fish, using your favorite recipe.

This delightful fish has come to us only recently from Kenya. The fish whole is very, very big — about four or five feet long. It is cleaned, skinned, and boned, and then the flesh is cut into large steaks. It can be found in most supermarkets. If you don't have it in your area yet, be sure to ask your grocer to get it for you. Many mash-gichim go to Kenya to supervise the preparation of the fish. It comes to us frozen in family-size pieces.

I have been experimenting with all kinds of recipes, and so far my favorite is this one that I got from Fannie Schwartz.

Salmon Quiche

1 **piecrust**

2 **onions**, sautéed

1 16 oz. can salmon

½ cup mayonnaise

1 Tbsp. **prepared mustard**

1 Tbsp. **lemon juice**

2 **eggs**, beaten

½ cup **milk**

salt and **pepper** to taste

Place piecrust in a dish with a layer of sautéed onions. Mix rest of ingredients and add to piecrust. Bake at 375° for 30 minutes.

Parve cream or water may be used instead of milk.

Moroccan Fish and Potatoes

1 Tbsp. **paprika**

½ cup **corn oil**

4 medium **potatoes**, peeled and sliced thin

2 small **hot red peppers**, sliced lengthwise, with seeds removed

1½ lb. **fish fillet or steaks**

1 whole head **garlic**

1 tsp. **salt**

1 – 2 tsp. **paprika**

¼ – ½ cup **fresh coriander**, chopped coarsely

In a heavy skillet or dutch oven-type pot, layer the sliced potatoes and sprinkle with 1 Tbsp. paprika and oil. Place sliced peppers on top, then slices of fish. Slice each garlic clove in half lengthwise and scatter over fish. Sprinkle salt on next, then 1 tsp. paprika. Lastly, spread coriander over everything.

Add water up to middle of fish layers and boil on medium heat until water is reduced to just under fish layer, shaking pan occasionally.

Unique Lasagna al Forno

1 16 oz. pkg. **lasagna noodles**

1 large **onion**, chopped finely

4 Tbsp. **margarine**

4 Tbsp. **all-purpose flour**

2 Tbsp. **parve chicken-flavored soup powder**

1½ cups **milk**

3 – 4 cups shredded **cheese**

½ tsp. **ground nutmeg**

½ cup **white wine**

Parmesan cheese for garnishing

Cook noodles and drain well. Cook onion in margarine until soft but not browned. Blend in flour. Remove from heat and gradually stir in soup powder and milk. Return to high heat and cook, stirring until it boils. Stir in 3 – 4 cups cheese, nutmeg, and white wine. Remove from heat.

Layer lasagna noodles with cheese sauce in a baking dish. Bake uncovered at 350° for 20 – 30 minutes.

Spoon portions of Lasagna onto individual plates. Top generously with homemade Spaghetti Sauce and Parmesan.

Blintze Soufflé

6 **blintzes** (frozen or homemade)

2 Tbsp. **butter**, melted

2 **eggs**

½ pint **sour cream**

2 Tbsp. **sugar**

2 Tbsp. **orange juice**

sugar and **cinnamon** (optional)

Place blintzes in a casserole and sprinkle melted butter over them. Blend remaining ingredients and pour over blintzes. Sprinkle with sugar and cinnamon.

Bake at 350° until lightly browned on top.

This is an extravagant way of serving blintzes, but I promise you the dieters in the crowd will forget the calories and enjoy every mouthful.

RICE and GRAINS

Brown Rice

2 cups **brown rice**

4½ cups **water**

½ tsp. **salt**

1 Tbsp. **oil**

Cook everything together for 20 – 30 minutes, then turn off flame and let stand until ready to use. I have recently started making my rice in the microwave and find it much easier. Consult your microwave instruction book for exact timing. Hint for microwaving: start with very hot water.

Jedda Rice and Lentils

1 large **onion**

1 cup **lentils**

3½ cups **water**

3 cups **rice**

Chop onion and sauté until golden. Add lentils and sauté for another 2 minutes. Add water and rice.

When the water boils, mix everything again and put the pot on a *blech* or over a very low flame. Allow it to simmer until rice is done. This can be made in the microwave after water is added.

Couscous

STEAMER METHOD:

Empty packet of **couscous** into a bowl and add 1 cup **water**. Mix and let stand for a few minutes. Put strainer on top of the pot that has the sauce in it. Spoon couscous into strainer. Steam for 20 minutes. Couscous should be soft. Top with sauce.

PAN METHOD:

Boil 2 cups **water** and 1 cup **oil** in frying pan. Add **seasoning** (powdered soup mix may be used). Let it come to a boil and turn down fire. Put in packet of **couscous** and stir well. Cover and let stand for 10 minutes. Mix with a fork, adding some sauce. Mix again and cover for another 5 minutes. Make sure couscous is soft.

Serve with sauce.

Sauce

1 **onion**, chopped

1 lb. **meat, chicken, or lamb**

2 **carrots**, diced

1 **cabbage**, shredded

2 **squash**, cubed

½ cup **chick peas**, soaked overnight

1 cup **water**

Sauté onion, then add meat and vegetables. Add chick peas and water. Cook for 1 hour on low flame.

I am one of those very lucky people who have been able to make good friends wherever I choose to live. Having moved twenty-seven times in the forty-nine years that we have been married, I've had the opportunity to make many friends. Here in the Old City of Jerusalem, I not only have friends, but I now have more family than I started out with. The community is a close one — each person cares about the other. We very often have Shabbos meals with a local Sephardi family, the Mashon, and the culinary delights that Selma Mashon cooks always get me in trouble. My husband invariably says, "Hon, why can't you make rice like this?" "Nate, I do make rice like this — it just doesn't come out the same." Each and every one of us develops our very own style in cooking. One has a heavier hand, another is lighter on the seasoning. Measurements are often the same, but not exactly the same. Another cook may not taste the food until it is served. Some are more adventurous with spices, some less. Put yourself into your cooking — then it has to be good.

Kasha Varnishkes (Buckwheat and Bow Ties)

2 cups **kasha** (buckwheat groats)

1 **egg**, beaten

1 **onion**, chopped and sautéed

salt and **pepper**

3 – 4 cups **boiling water**

8 oz. **bow tie noodles**, boiled

Heat a large skillet and add kasha. Pour egg into skillet and stir vigorously until kasha is coated and slightly browned. Add boiling water and stir. Cover skillet and let cook, checking frequently, until all the water is absorbed. Add onion and seasoning. Add bow ties and toss. At this point you can add any gravy that you have, or serve as is.

This is an old-time favorite in many Jewish homes.

Sephardi Rice with Pasta

1 cup **orzo** (tiny egg-shaped pasta)

1 Tbsp. **oil**

¼ tsp. **salt**

2½ cups (or more) **water**, or 3 cups if brown rice is used

2 cups **rice** (white or brown)

Brown pasta in oil and salt. Add water, and when boiling put in rice. When it has begun to boil again, reduce flame to very low, stirring once or twice until water is all absorbed (approx. 20 minutes).

KUGELS

Apple Cinnamon Noodle Kugel

1 16 oz. pkg. **medium noodles**, cooked

4 oz. **butter or margarine**

6 **eggs**, separated

½ cup **sugar**

1 tsp. **vanilla**

3 or 4 sliced **apples or** 1 medium can **pineapple**
    (crushed, chunks, or slices)

½ cup **pineapple juice**

juice of 1 **lemon** (optional)

raisins and **cinnamon**

Preheat oven to 350°.

In a large bowl, mix hot noodles with butter or margarine and add egg yolks, sugar, vanilla, apples, or pineapple plus pineapple juice and lemon juice. Fold in egg whites that have been whipped into soft white peaks. Fold in raisins. Sprinkle the top generously with cinnamon.

Bake for 1 hour.

Using these amounts I find that a 9" x 13" pan is too small for the kugel. I usually manage to make a small kugel with the overflow and put it in the freezer. Actually, you can safely divide this recipe into any size pans you have. It freezes very well and is heated through quickly in the microwave.

This is a very special recipe and can be made with almost any fruit you desire. I often make it with a can of fruit cocktail or peaches or apricots. A container of sour cream or cottage cheese added to the mixture makes it a dairy delight.

Every Jewish woman has a special kugel recipe that most likely was handed down from her Bubby. Here are some of the traditional kugels. Let your creative talents come forth — use your intuition and create your very own favorite recipe.

A savory kugel is always a special side dish and can be made with noodles or vegetables. There are a variety of recipes here. Choose one that will be a complement to your main course.

Applesauce Noodle Kugel

6 **eggs**, separated

4 oz. **margarine**

1 cup **sugar**

1 tsp. **vanilla**

1 16 oz. pkg. **medium noodles**, cooked and drained

1 16 oz. can (or equivalent of homemade) **applesauce**

Beat egg whites until they form peaks, and set aside.

Melt margarine in a 9" x 13" pan. In a bowl, mix egg yolks and sugar lightly. Add vanilla. Fold in noodles and applesauce. Then fold in egg whites. Pour into pan, mixing lightly to combine margarine.

Topping

2 cups crushed **cornflakes**

1 cup **brown sugar**

cinnamon to taste

Combine ingredients. Sprinkle over noodle mixture, patting the topping down. Bake at 350° for 1 hour

This recipe came from two very special brothers — twins — who were studying at Aish HaTorah. I had just served a kugel, and one of them said, "Almost like my mother's — she makes a noodle kugel with applesauce." My reply was: "Tell your mom to send me her recipe." I go to great lengths to have my boys feel at home here. I got the recipe and made it the next time Phil and Rob Shore came for dinner. It was a taste of home for them, and we all loved it.

Broccoli Kugel

2 pkgs. **frozen broccoli**

2 heaping Tbsp. **onion soup mix**

¾ cup **mayonnaise**

3 **eggs**, beaten

¼ cup **flour**

salt and **pepper** to taste

Place broccoli in a casserole and mix remainder of ingredients in a bowl. Pour over broccoli and bake at 350° for 35 – 40 minutes.

Any cooked or partially cooked vegetable can be used for this tasty gourmet kugel. I have used 2 cups sliced zucchini or mixed vegetables with great success.

Carrot Kugel

3 cups shredded **carrots**

2 **eggs**

½ cup **brown sugar**

8 oz. **margarine**

juice and **rind** of 1 **lemon**

2 cups **flour**

1½ tsp. **baking powder**

1 tsp. **baking soda**

½ tsp. **salt**

1 tsp. **vanilla**

½ tsp. **cinnamon**

nuts and **raisins** (optional)

Mix all ingredients and pour into a well-greased 9" x 13" pan or a bundt or angel food pan and bake at 350° for 45 – 50 minutes.

This unusual carrot kugel can be served warm with dinner or cold and iced for a delightful dessert. An orange butter cream icing is recommended (see icing for Special Occasion Cake)

Carrot Vegetable Ring

2 **eggs**, separated

8 oz. **margarine**

1 cup **brown sugar**

1 Tbsp. **lemon juice**

1 cup cooked **carrots**, mashed

1½ cups **flour**

1 tsp. **baking powder**

1 tsp. **baking soda**

cinnamon and **nutmeg** to taste

Whip egg whites until peaks form and set aside.

Mix rest of ingredients and fold in **egg** whites. Pour into a tube pan. Bake at 350° for 30 – 35 minutes.

Serve warm.

Cauliflower Casserole

1 average-size **cauliflower**

2 – 3 **eggs**

½ tsp. **salt**

¼ tsp. **pepper**

½ cup **matzah meal**

¼ cup grated **Parmesan cheese** (optional)

Cook and mash cauliflower. Add rest of ingredients and place in a casserole.

Bake at 450° for 15 minutes and then at 350° until it is browned.

Chinese Kugel

8 oz. **medium noodles**, cooked

1 **onion**, chopped

2 oz. **margarine**

1 pkg. **frozen broccoli**, defrosted

2 Tbsp. **onion soup mix**

3 **eggs**, beaten

½ cup **parve cream**

1 can sliced **water chestnuts** (optional)

Sauté onions in margarine. Mix all ingredients together and bake at 350° for 45 minutes.

Chopped Liver Kugel

3 large **onions**, chopped

1 Tbsp. **oil**

1 lb. **medium noodles**, cooked

½ lb. **fresh mushrooms**, sliced

8 oz. **baby beef liver**

4 **eggs**

salt and **pepper** to taste

Fry onions in oil until golden brown. Add to cooked noodles. Sauté mushrooms and add to noodles. Broil liver and grate or put through a grinder or processor. Add to noodles. Beat eggs and add to noodles. Salt and pepper to taste.

Bake at 350° until browned for 1 hour.

For the vegetarians in the crowd, use Mock Chopped Liver and sauté additional onions and mushrooms.

Yerushalmi Kugel

1 cup **sugar**

½ cup **oil**

1 lb. **fine noodles**

1 **egg**, beaten

1½ tsp. **salt**

1 tsp. **pepper**

Cook and drain noodles thoroughly.

Cook sugar in oil, caramelizing and stirring constantly. Add noodles when sugar becomes a light brown syrup and mix thoroughly — they will tend to harden the caramelized mixture and therefore it is necessary to stir vigorously as soon as you add the noodles. Add egg, salt, and pepper.

Bake at 350° for 1½ hours.

Keep on the *blech* overnight.

I usually make this on Wednesday and refrigerate it to be baked when the oven is being used for other baking. This unusual kugel is a delicacy to be eaten on Shabbos — at a kiddush or as a luncheon appetizer.

Potato Kugel

2 lbs. (or more) **potatoes**

2 medium **onions**, chopped

6 large **eggs**, well beaten

⅓ cup **matzah meal**

⅓ cup **oil**

salt and **pepper** to taste

Grate potatoes and let them stand for 5 minutes. Pour off excess water. Mix in onions, eggs, and matzah meal. Add oil. Salt and pepper to taste. Pour into a greased pan.
    Bake at 350° for 45 minutes to 1 hour.

Savory Noodle Kugel

1 **onion**, chopped

¼ lb. **mushrooms**, fresh or canned

1 16 oz. pkg. **medium noodles**

4 **eggs**

4 oz. **margarine**

salt and **pepper** to taste

Sauté onion and mushrooms. Mix in rest of ingredients and pour into a greased 9" x 13" pan. Bake at 350° for 1 hour.

PIES

Piecrust #1

2¼ cups **flour**

¾ tsp. **salt**

8 oz. **margarine**

6 Tbsp. **ice water**

Mix in food processor until dough cleans the sides of the bowl and sticks to the blade.

Hand method: Mix flour, salt, and margarine, until it is in tiny crumbs. Gradually add ice water until dough forms a solid ball.

Refrigerate for 15 minutes. Cut dough in half and roll out each piece to fit a 9" pie pan. Makes two 9" pie crusts.

Piecrust #2

3 cups **flour**

1 tsp. **salt**

8 oz. **butter or margarine**

1 **egg**

5 Tbsp. **cold water**

Mix all ingredients in food processor, dripping the water in until the dough forms a ball around the blade.

Hand method: Mix flour and salt. Cut in shortening. Beat egg and water. Add to flour mixture and mix into a smooth ball.

Makes two 9" pie crusts.

Cookie Crumb Piecrust

1 pkg. **tea biscuits or graham crackers or any cookies**

8 oz. **margarine**

Crumble cookies and margarine together in food processor. Pat into a pie pan and fill with your favorite filling. Bake at 350°. This crust may be made ahead of time and used as needed. I try to keep a supply in the freezer.

> *I often use the Cookie Crumb Piecrust for my pies and cheesecakes, and also as a topping for fruit pies. Leftover cake makes a great crumb piecrust.*

Meringue Piecrust

3 **egg whites**

6 Tbsp. **sugar**

nuts and/or coconut

Beat egg whites and gradually add sugar until stiff. Fold in nuts and/or coconut. Grease a pie plate and place the meringue in the center. With a spatula, spread the meringue evenly around the pan and up the sides.

Bake in a medium oven until lightly brown. Remove from oven and allow to cool. I have found this a very useful piecrust, especially good for the Chocolate Mousse Pie.

> *Recently I made this crust with oatmeal nut crumbs that I had left from a batch of Crunchies. It was great.*

Banana or Coconut Cream Pie

2 cups **milk**

1/3 cup **flour**

1/2 cup **sugar**

1/8 tsp. **salt**

3 **eggs**, separated

2 Tbsp. **margarine or butter**

1 1/2 tsp. **vanilla**

1 cup **coconut or** 2 sliced **bananas**, or a combination of both

1 **piecrust**, baked

6 Tbsp. **sugar**

Scald milk in a double boiler or over a very low flame. Stir in flour, sugar, and salt. Continue to cook, stirring constantly, until mixture thickens. Take a little of the mixture and stir it into the egg yolks, then add them back into the pot. Allow this to cook for 2 minutes on a very low flame. Then add margarine or butter and vanilla.

Put coconut or bananas directly on a baked pie-crust. Pour custard over it all, mixing a little if coconut is used (or coconut can be mixed into the custard before putting it into the crust.)

Beat egg whites with sugar until a meringue is formed. Spoon over the pie and bake at 450° for 5 – 10 minutes. It can also be put under the broiler — watch carefully so as not to burn the meringue.

This is a specialty of the house — but not made too often because it can only be eaten after a dairy meal. Some of my boys like coconut only and others like banana only — then there are those who like the combination. I often get into trouble trying to figure out which one likes which pie.

Once, Moshe Baruch, Elana, and Shira Naomi (then 2 1/2) came to Israel for the holidays and I was busy making all my son's favorite recipes. Coconut Cream Pie won the Dessert of the Visit award. Moshe actually ate half of a pie and could have eaten more.

Pecan Pie

1 unbaked 9" **pie shell**

1 cup **corn syrup**

1 cup **dark brown sugar**

¼ tsp. **salt**

3 oz. **butter or margarine**, melted

1 tsp. **vanilla**

3 **eggs**, lightly beaten

1 heaping cup **pecan halves**

Preheat oven to 350°. Combine syrup, sugar, salt, butter, and vanilla, mixing well. Add eggs. Place pecans into pie shell and pour mixture over them. Bake for 45 minutes.

Chocolate Pecan Pie

1 **piecrust**, unbaked

2 **eggs**

1 cup **sugar**

$1/2$ cup **flour**

4 oz. **butter or margarine**, melted

1 tsp. **vanilla**

1 cup **pecans**

6 oz. **chocolate chips**

Beat eggs. Blend in sugar, flour, butter, and vanilla. Stir in pecans and chocolate chips.

Pour into unbaked piecrust and bake at 325° for 50 minutes. Cool. Garnish with whipped cream or ice cream.

Chocolate Mousse Pie with Meringue Crust

Crust

3 **egg whites**

$1/2$ cup **sugar**

$1/2$ cup chopped **almonds**

$1/2$ cup grated **coconut**

Beat egg whites with sugar until stiff peaks form. Fold in almonds and coconut. Bake in greased pie pan at 375° until peaks are slightly browned. Remove from oven and cool.

Filling

8 oz. **chocolate**

1 cup **parve whip or heavy cream**

1 jigger (1 – $1/2$ oz.) **brandy**

Melt chocolate and let cool a bit. Whip cream until peaks form. Carefully fold chocolate into cream. Add brandy and spoon mousse into piecrust. Refrigerate until served.

The *"Devilish Mousse Pie"* — *A Bubby Irma story by Moshe Wilshensky*

One Shabbos about ten years ago, Irma served a large Mousse Pie. By Sunday morning, there was a little less than two-thirds of the pie left, sitting innocently in the fridge. Moshe (Irma's son) and I were sitting in another room minding our own business, when all of a sudden the pie came to our minds. We remembered how deliciously rich it tasted, and we decided we must have some. The warning from Irma not to touch it because she was expecting guests faded in our minds. However, we still planned it as a covert operation. We organized it as if we were liberating a fugitive in a hostile country. Moshe, being the elder and also the son of the house, went off on the mission. He came back successful, with the pie and two forks. The pie had a rich chocolate mousse filling, with a very even texture, and it was surrounded by a delicious moist crumb crust. We enjoyed that pie so much, but we knew finishing the whole pie would be fatal (Irma would have definitely killed us) so we decided to leave a small piece in the pan. Reluctantly, we stopped eating the pie, and a lonely sliver lay there in a practically empty dish.

The next move in our covert operation was to return the contraband to its rightful place. Once again, Moshe was the one for the task. When Moshe returned we figured it was over. Like so many criminals, we thought we would never be caught. Irma would find it when we weren't around and by the time we would see her all would be fine. Boy, were we wrong!

Moshe and I continued what we were doing without noticing that Irma's guests had arrived. Then it all happened in slow motion: We heard Irma offer everyone pie, then step over to the kitchen and open the refrigerator. At that point we knew our goose was cooked. Irma reached in to get what she thought was to be a few servings of pie and discovered the one serving that was left was thin enough to pass Weight Watchers charts. In that short time of her walking from the kitchen to the room we were in, we acted bravely, and, as any guilty party would do, frantically tried to hide, but there was nothing in the room to hide behind or under. In desperation, I moved the couch away from the wall and crawled into the space, and Moshe tried to jam himself in a closet full of boxes.

Well, needless to say Irma discovered us. We were guilty as could be, and the first thing out of Moshe's mouth was "The devil made me do it!" Since then there have been many pies that Moshe and I have enjoyed "legally," but that story always comes to mind when I think of Irma's "devilishly good Mousse Pie."

Coconut Parve Pie

3 **eggs**, well-beaten

1 cup **sugar**

1 cup **coconut**, grated — fresh is special

1 Tbsp. **vinegar**

1 tsp. **vanilla**

2 oz. **margarine**, melted

Mix well and put into unbaked pie shell. Bake at 350°
for 1 hour.

Impossible Pie

2 cups **milk**

8 oz. **margarine**

2 tsp. **vanilla**

4 **eggs**

1 cup **sugar**

½ cup **flour**

¼ tsp. **salt**

1 cup **coconut**

Preheat oven to 350°. Place all ingredients in blender and
combine thoroughly. Grease and flour a 10" pie pan and
pour in mixture.

Bake for 30 – 40 minutes until set. It makes its own
crust as it cooks. Serve at room temperature.

CAKES and ICINGS

Apple Cake #1

8 oz. **butter or margarine**

½ cup **sugar or apple juice concentrate**

1 **egg**

1 tsp. **vanilla**

1¾ cups **flour**

¼ tsp. **salt**

3 tsp. **baking powder**

⅓ cup **milk or parve cream**

2 or 3 **apples**

½ cup **brown sugar**

½ tsp. **cinnamon**

Cream butter and sugar. Beat egg in until light and fluffy. Add vanilla. Add flour, salt, and baking powder alternately with milk. Put mixture in a greased, medium square pan. Peel, core, and cut apples in thin sections and arrange in rows on cake. Mix brown sugar with cinnamon and sprinkle over apples.

Bake at 400° for 35 – 40 minutes. Best served warm with topping of whipped cream or ice cream.

This cake stays moist and is delicious. Double the recipe for a 9" x 13" pan.

Apple Cake #2

4 cups finely sliced **apples**

⅓ cup **sugar or apple juice concentrate**

3 Tbsp. **cinnamon**

3 cups **flour**

1 Tbsp. **baking powder**

½ tsp. **salt**

2 cups **sugar**

1 cup **oil**

1 Tbsp. **vanilla**

4 **eggs**

¼ cup **orange or pineapple juice**

Mix apples, ⅓ cup sugar, and cinnamon. In a separate bowl, mix flour, baking powder, salt, and 2 cups sugar. Make a well and add oil, vanilla, eggs, and juice. Mix well. Pour into tube pan in layers — first cake mixture, then apples, then cake and more apples. Bake at 350° for 1-1½ hours.

Apple Crisp

The Apple Crisp Discovery

It seems as if it were a million years ago — or was it just yesterday — that Vicki was 8 years old and I brought her new baby brother home from the hospital. She was so excited and wanted to help wherever she could. We let her make dinner. She and Debi (5½ years old) made the greatest green mashed potatoes, eggs, and a salad.

For dessert they made a surprise: Apple Crisp. They had the recipe in their junior cookbook. It was delicious and became a favorite in the House of Charles.

This quick and delicious recipe saves the day when we have unexpected guests. It is easy to assemble and can be served as soon as it comes out of the oven. When the apple season is over, I use fresh peaches.

It is not advisable to make this recipe on Wednesday. With the amount of traffic that comes through the House of Charles, there is nothing left for Shabbos.

6 **apples** — green sour apples are my favorite, but any apple may be used. If sweeter apples are used, add lemon juice.

1 cup **brown sugar or** ¼ cup **sugar** plus ½ cup **apple juice concentrate**

1 cup **flour**

1 cup **oatmeal**

8 oz. **butter or margarine**

Slice apples and place in a 9" x 13" pan. Sprinkle with cinnamon. Mix sugar, flour, oatmeal, and margarine, and sprinkle on top of apples. Bake at 350° for 40 minutes. Delicious served warm with cream or ice cream.

If you are short of apples, a can of applesauce with a bit of cinnamon can be added to the sliced apples.

A Bubby Tale

One evening when Natie was working late, I decided to surprise him and make apple strudel. We lived in three rooms in back of our mini supermarket in Arlington, Virginia. I started baking about 7 P.M.— sure that I would be finished before he closed the store. At 1 A.M. I finally took the strudel out of the oven — the aroma was pure perfume, apples and cinnamon. It looked beautiful. I cut the first piece, anxious to taste this delicacy, and could not believe how awful it was. It was hard and inedible. In anger and frustration, I left the kitchen just as it was and went to sleep. The next morning, after throwing it all out and cleaning up, I reread the recipe. I had done everything exactly right — except for turning the page. The recipe went on to say: roll out dough as thin as possible, and then put your hands under it and stretch the dough until it doubles in size. From that time on, I bought apple strudel in bakeries or restaurants, until one day I discovered a Bubby recipe for mock strudel.

Mock Apple Strudel

The trick

1 pkg. **prepared piecrust mix or dough**

Roll out dough as thin as possible.

The filling

6 **apples**

1 cup **sugar**, with 2 – 3 tsp. **cinnamon** mixed in

1 cup **raisins**

½ cup **coconut** (optional)

Grate apples and mix with sugar, cinnamon, raisins, and coconut. Spread mixture on **dough** and roll up like a jelly roll. You can make large rolls for dessert, or small rolls sprinkled with powdered sugar to go into paper cups on a cookie tray.

Babka

4¼ cups **flour**

8 oz. **margarine**, melted

3 **eggs**, separated

1¼ cups **sugar**

1 tsp. **vanilla**

½ cup **milk or water**

½ cup **sour cream or parve cream**

4 oz. fresh or dried **yeast**

¼ cup **warm water**

cinnamon, **nuts**, **raisins**, **coconut**

jelly or preserves

Put flour into a bowl and make a well. Add margarine, egg yolks, ¼ cup sugar, vanilla, milk, sour cream, and yeast dissolved in water. Mix into smooth dough. Refrigerate in a covered bowl for several hours or overnight.

I usually make a good supply of this dough and keep it in an airtight jar without the jelly. It can be used for many cakes, toppings, or fillings.

Roll dough out on a floured board or table to a 30"x24" rectangle (the larger side will be the bottom). It usually takes up half my kitchen table. The thinner the dough, the better the babka. Whip egg whites with remaining cup of sugar into a meringue till stiff peaks form. Spread meringue over dough, as if icing it, leaving a 1" border at the top. Sprinkle meringue generously with cinnamon, nuts, raisins, coconut, and a line of jam or jelly in the center of the dough.

Roll dough into a large roll, starting at the bottom and rolling up. Near the top, bring the dough forward and wrap around the roll. Cut into 6 even pieces. Place pieces into a well-greased tube pan, cut sides down. Cover with a damp cloth and let rise 1 – 1½ hours.

Bake at 400° for 10 minutes, then lower oven to 350° for another 40 minutes. Do not overbake!

The Babka Story

Thirty-five years ago we lived in Worcester, Massachusetts. It was there that my career in cooking started. A very dear friend gave me this recipe, and the first time I made it I knew I had a winner.

Two uncles came for a visit and I wanted to impress them. It was an overwhelming success. That evening I had to make the dough again to show my aunts how to make it, and the next morning I rolled it out so they could see how it was done. It is really so simple — but neither of them ever made it. I became the babka-maker in the family. When we left America to live in Israel, Debi, daughter number 2, took over my job so that a babka is at every family function.

Banana Cake

2¼ cups **flour**

1¼ cups **sugar** or ¾ cups **apple juice concentrate**

2½ tsp. **baking powder**

¾ tsp. **baking soda**

½ tsp. **salt**

4 oz. **margarine**

1½ cups mashed **ripe bananas**

1 tsp. **vanilla**

2 **eggs**

¼ cup **orange juice** (optional)

Beat all ingredients and pour into a greased pan. I have made this cake in a 10" tube pan, loaf pans, layer cake pans, or a 9" x 13" pan. Bake at 350° for 35 minutes. Tube pans and loaf pans need 45 minutes.

Chocolate chips may added to the batter. The real trick to this cake is to have very ripe bananas.

Hint: *If bananas are not ripe, peel and freeze them overnight. When they defrost they are soft and give the cake a rich flavor.*

Carrot Cake

4 oz. **margarine or butter**

½ cup **honey**

1 Tbsp. **cinnamon**

¼ tsp. **salt**

2 **eggs**

1 cup coarsely grated **carrots**

½ cup **chopped nuts**

1¼ cups **whole wheat flour**

1½ tsp. **baking powder**

Cream margarine or butter until soft. Add honey and mix well. Stir in cinnamon and salt. Add eggs and mix well. Add carrots and nuts and mix again.

Sift flour and baking powder and add to batter gradually. Use an 8" x 8" baking pan or a loaf pan. Bake at 350° for 30 minutes.

This carrot cake is great with frosting — a white frosting is ideal (see Special Occasion Cake icing).

Special Occasion Cake

2 cups **sugar**

1 cup **oil**

4 **eggs**

1 cup **orange juice**

3 cups **flour**

3 tsp. **baking powder**

2 tsp. **vanilla**

Mix all ingredients in order given, adding eggs one at a time. Use double the recipe to make two 12" layers. Bake at 350° for approx. 35 minutes or until top is golden. Icing or jam can be spread between the layers.

Icing

6 oz. **margarine**

1 lb. **powdered sugar**, sifted

2 tsp. **vanilla or mint flavoring**

2 Tbsp. **water or orange juice**

food coloring (optional)

Cream margarine and add sugar slowly. Add flavoring, water, and food coloring, if wanted. Orange juice may be used instead of flavorings. Makes 2 cups of icing.

The pleasure of taking a perfectly baked cake out of the oven can best be described as pure joy, and decorating a beautiful cake brings out all our latent artistic talents.

Timna, granddaughter number two, wanted to celebrate her bas mitzvah here in Jerusalem. We had the party on the second day of Chanukah in our house. The menu for over one hundred guests became a challenge. It was such fun.

We served a buffet of blintzes, burekas, quiches (spinach and cheese), Marinated Cabbage Salad, Unique Lasagna al Forno, doughnuts, pickles, Marinated Mushrooms and Carrots, Babka, Rugelach, Heavenly Bits, and Grace Abramovitz's pecan tarts.

And of course, we had an unforgettable birthday cake — the Special Occasion Cake, in three tiers! Carol Topf, my very dear friend, supplied the recipe and her talents in cake decorating, and her set of octagon-shaped baking pans. I baked the layers and froze them. The night before the party we all iced the cake: yellow icing with pink roses and green leaves.

We had such fun decorating it until 2 in the morning. Andreia, who is now 9, hopefully will have the same for her bas mitzvah.

Daughter number two, Debi, came for the bas mitzvah with her two children, Aaron Michael and Elyse. It was a wonderful time in the House of Charles. My family and my adopted family kept the house jumping.

Easy Cake

8 oz. **butter or margarine**

1 cup **sugar**

1 cup **sour cream, yogurt, or parve cream or orange juice**

1 tsp. **vanilla**

1 tsp. **lemon juice**

3 **eggs**

2½ cups **self-rising flour**

Beat everything together until well blended.

Filling (optional)

½ cup **sugar**

1 tsp. **cinnamon**

1 cup **chopped pecans**

½ tsp. **nutmeg**

Pour half the batter into a pan and sprinkle filling mixture over it, saving a little filling for the top. Cover with rest of batter. Sprinkle remaining mix on top of cake.

Bake at 350° for 45 – 50 minutes.

VARIATIONS

Leave out filling and ice cake with Broiled Coconut Icing right after it comes out of the oven.

I call this cake the building cake — I can add nuts and coconut or fruit, or a special icing, and transform the cake into a completely different one.

Special Poppy Seed Cake

Use the **Easy Cake** recipe without filling, and blend 4 oz. **poppy seeds** into the batter.

Coffee Cake

12 oz. **margarine**

1½ cups **sugar**

4 **eggs**, separated

2 cups **flour**

3 tsp. **baking powder**

½ tsp. **salt**

½ cup **milk or water**

1 tsp. **vanilla**

½ cup **nuts**

½ cup **coconut**

½ cup **chocolate syrup**

Beat egg whites until stiff and set aside.

Cream margarine and sugar. Add yolks and beat well. Sift flour with baking powder and salt, and add to mixture alternately with liquid. Add vanilla and fold in egg whites. Pour half the mixture into greased angel food pan that has been sprinkled with half of nuts and coconut mixture. Swirl in chocolate syrup and pour remaining batter over. Sprinkle top with remaining nuts and coconut. Bake at 350° for 1 hour.

Hot Milk Sponge Cake

1 scant cup **flour**

1 tsp. **baking powder**

¼ tsp. **salt**

2 Tbsp. **butter or margarine**

½ cup **hot milk or parve cream**

2 **eggs**

1 cup **sugar**

1 tsp. **vanilla**

Sift dry ingredients. Add butter to hot milk and keep hot. Beat eggs with sugar for 4-5 minutes. Add sifted ingredients to egg mixture and stir until just blended. Stir in hot milk mixture and vanilla. Bake in large loaf pan at 350° for 30-35 minutes. Cool in pan for 15 minutes. Ice with Broiled Coconut Icing.

This cake with its very special icing used to travel the length and breadth of the United States. During World War II, my sister Helen sent this cake at least once a month to my brother on his army base. Herb was the most popular soldier on the base the day that the cake arrived. It is another family treasure.

Cookie Nut Cake

Dark, moist, and chunky. This is a Nina Spiro recipe.

8 oz. **butter or margarine**

1¾ cups **sugar**

6 **eggs**

3 cups **vanilla wafer crumbs or** 3 cups **biscuit crumbs**
   (or any cookie crumbs). If biscuit crumbs are
   used add 2 tsp. **vanilla.**

7 oz. **shredded coconut**

1 – 2 cups **chopped pecans**

powdered sugar

Cream butter and sugar until light and fluffy. Beat in eggs
one at a time. Add cookie crumbs, coconut, and pecans.
Pour batter into a prepared tube pan or a bundt pan. Bake
at 350° for 1 hour or until cake pulls away from the pan
and a tester inserted in the center comes out clean. Cool
cake in pan for 10 minutes and remove to a cake plate.
Dust with powdered sugar just before serving.

VARIATION

Variations can be made — use your creative talents. I
   have used all kinds of crumbs. Leftover cake adds
   yet another flavor. Use brownies (may be flavored
   with mint) for a fabulous cake.

HINT: *I serve this cake very often in my entertaining. It is
another recipe that can be moist even if overbaked.
Pour any juice over the hot cake as soon as it comes
out of the oven and cover until it cools.*

Orange Juice Cake

6 **eggs**, separated

1½ cups **sugar**

1 cup **orange juice**

½ cup **oil**

2½ cups **self-rising flour**

grated **lemon rind**

Beat egg whites into soft peaks. Combine all remaining
ingredients. Fold in egg whites. Bake in tube pan, loaf
pan, 9" x 13" pan, or 2 round layer pans at 350° for 35 –
40 minutes.

Fruit and Nut Cake

— I always make this cake to keep him in a happy mood. He will never own up to this, but it is true.

8 – 9 **eggs**, separated

2 cups **sugar**

12 oz. **margarine**

2¼ cups **flour**

2 tsp. **vanilla**

1 tsp. **lemon juice**

Beat egg whites stiff and set aside. Beat egg yolks with rest of ingredients. Fold in egg whites. Then fold in:

1 cup **nuts**

1 cup **raisins**

1 cup **apricots**, chopped

cinnamon to taste

Can be made in loaf pans, or in an angel food tin. Bake at 350° for approx. 1 hour.

I first made this recipe without the fruit and nuts, and it was great. The next time I was in one of my creative moods, I added the fruit and nuts. Natie was so excited over it that he said he could eat it every day — it became his special cake. Whenever I know that I have invited too many guests for Shabbos — or made too much food

Kenya's Rich Raisin Cake

2 ¼ cups **sugar**

10 oz. **butter**

6 **eggs**

2 Tbsp. **instant coffee**, dissolved in a little **water**

3 Tbsp. **brandy**

2 tsp. grated **lemon peel**

2 tsp. grated **orange peel**

2 Tbsp. chopped **cherries**

2 oz. chopped **cashew nuts**

2 – 3 lbs. **raisins**

1½ cups **flour**

Mix first 3 ingredients and then add following 7 ingredients. Mix in flour.

Bake in loaf pans lined with waxed paper at 350° for 1 hour. Lower oven to 275° and bake for 3 more hours.

In Kenya, Mama Szlaypak is famous for her raisin cake. She is in her eighties and still bakes it for every occasion. We bring home all kinds of treasures from Kenya, but Mama's raisin cake gets the most raves.

Yeast Coffee Cake

2 oz. **yeast**

1 cup **lukewarm milk, parve cream or water**

2 tsp. **sugar**

4 cups **flour**

5 **egg yolks**

pinch of **salt**

¼ cup **vanilla sugar**

4 oz. **butter or margarine**, melted

2 tsp. **cookie crumbs**

1 cup **chopped walnuts**

grated **lemon rind**

Mix yeast with ¼ cup milk and 2 tsp. of sugar and let stand.

Make a well in the flour and add egg yolks, salt, vanilla sugar, and yeast mixture. Mix and slowly add half the melted butter. Add more flour if necessary.

Grease an angel food tin and sprinkle with cookie crumbs and some chopped walnuts. Roll dough out thick and cut into rounds. Dip each round into melted butter and lay it out in the pan, so that rounds overlap each other. Sprinkle with nuts and drizzle rest of butter all over. This cake does not need to rise. Bake at 350° for 45 minutes.

Mystery Cake

1 can any **fruit pie filling** or homemade fruit pie filling

2 cups **flour**

1½ tsp. **baking soda**

1 tsp. **salt**

1 cup **sugar** (white or brown)

2 **eggs**, beaten

⅔ cup **oil or melted margarine**

1 tsp. **vanilla**

½ cup **chopped nuts** (optional)

1 tsp. **lemon juice** (optional)

Place ingredients in order given into a 9" x 13" pan and mix until blended. Bake at 350° for 40 minutes.
Sprinkle with powdered sugar to serve.

Lemon Loaf

4 oz. **butter or margarine**

1 cup **sugar**

2 **eggs**

grated **rind** of 1 **lemon**

1 ½ cups **flour**

1 tsp. **baking powder**

½ tsp. **salt**

⅔ cups **milk or parve cream**

Whip butter and gradually add sugar. Add remaining ingredients and bake at 350° for 1 hour in a loaf pan.

Syrup

¼ cup **honey**

⅓ cup **sugar**

juice of 1 **lemon** plus 2 tsp. **lemon juice**

Mix ingredients together. Pierce the cake while warm and pour syrup over it. Decorate with lemon slices.

Fridge Cake

Cookie Crumb Crust

1 8 oz. pkg. **tea biscuits or** other **cookies**

4 oz. **margarine or butter**

Crush cookie crumbs with margarine or butter in food processor. Pat into 9" spring form pan.

Filling

3 8 oz. **soft cream cheese**

4 oz. **margarine**

1 cup **sugar**

1 16 oz. can **crushed pineapple**

1½ pkgs. **gelatine**

1¼ cups **pineapple juice**

8 oz. **heavy cream**

Mix together in a bowl: cheese, margarine, sugar, and pineapple. Heat gelatine and juice. Add to cheese mixture with cream.

    Pour filling into crumb crust and refrigerate for several hours.

No-Crust Cheesecake

2 8 oz. pkgs. **cream cheese**

½ cup **sugar**

1 Tbsp. **lemon juice**

1 tsp. **vanilla**

½ cup **milk**

1 cup **sour cream**

2 **eggs**

lemon rind

Beat for 15 minutes. Bake at 350° for 15 minutes. Turn off heat and let cake stand in oven for 15 minutes longer.

Never-Fail Cheesecake

3 8 oz. pkgs. **cream cheese**

3 **eggs**

½ cup **sugar**

cookie crumb crust (see Fridge Cake recipe)

1 pint **sour cream**

¼ cup **sugar**

2 Tbsp. **vanilla**

Blend first 3 ingredients in blender or mixer on high speed until smooth and creamy. Pour into cookie crumb crust and bake in medium oven for 20 minutes only. Let cake cool a bit, and then mix last 3 ingredients together. Carefully spoon this on top of the warm cake and bake at 400° for 10 minutes only.

 This cheesecake can also be made in miniature cupcake tins. I use paper linings and spoon in the batter. It is an elegant addition to a tray of cookies.

Special Cheesecake

2¼ lbs. **cream cheese**

1¾ cups **sugar**

5 Tbsp. **flour**

2 Tbsp. **lemon juice**

½ tsp. **vanilla**

6 **eggs**

cookie crumb crust (see Fridge Cake recipe)

Mix first 6 ingredients in mixer, then fold in cream. Pour into crumb crust. Bake at 400° for 12 minutes, then turn the oven down to 300° and bake for 1 hour.

Easy Chiffon Cake

7 **egg whites**

½ tsp. **lemon juice**

2½ cups **flour**, sifted

1½ cups **sugar**

1 tsp. **baking powder**

1 tsp. **salt**

½ cup **oil**

7 – 8 **egg yolks**

¾ cup **cold water**

1 tsp. **vanilla**

Beat egg whites and lemon juice until stiff peaks form. Set aside. Sift dry ingredients into a large bowl. Make a well and add oil, egg yolks, water, and vanilla. Beat on high speed until smooth and shiny. Fold in egg whites. Bake at 325° for 1 – 1¼ hours.

Marble Chiffon Cake

Easy Chiffon Cake batter (previous recipe)

2 oz. **unsweetened chocolate**, melted

¼ cup **water**

2 Tbsp. **sugar**

Whip ingredients together until smooth. Cool. Take out one third cake batter and fold chocolate mixture into it. Put half the remaining batter into a pan, and swirl in the chocolate mixture. Cover with rest of batter.

Pineapple Chiffon Cake

To **Easy Chiffon Cake batter**, fold in ¾ of a 30 oz. can **crushed pineapple**, and use ¾ cup of its juice instead of water. Use remaining pineapple to make a white fluffy icing.

Icing

Mix remaining **crushed pineapple** with enough **powdered sugar** to make the icing spreadable, or use your favorite white icing and add remaining pineapple.

Chocolate Chip Chiffon Cake

A Chocolate Chip Chiffon Cake is delightful and can be served with or without an icing. Simply fold in 1 pkg. **chocolate chips** to **Easy Chiffon Cake batter**

One might ask, "What is this 'Bubby style?' " It is really very simple. I use any shortcut to a recipe. To become a favorite dish in my house, it has to be quick and easy.

Natie is so funny — when I make a particularly good meal, he always compliments me with a bit of sarcasm in his voice: "Hon, this is delicious — super, really super — but I know you'll never be able to make it the same way again." He is such a creature of habit — and I am just the opposite. I get bored with my menus and always like to make new dishes and experiment with the seasoning.

In cooking one has to be prepared for making mistakes and failures. I make many — but I am a very lucky lady: when I have a flop and have no time to make it over, I begin to improvise, and inevitably that is the dish that someone in the crowd wants the recipe for. Like the time that I made this absolutely delicious and beautiful chocolate mousse lady-finger cake in an angel food mold. It dropped out of my hands as I was taking it to the table and my guests were arriving momentarily. I quickly scooped it up into the platter again and squashed it all together (cleaning off any part that touched the floor of course) and iced the entire molded cake with another layer of whipped cream. What could be bad? I was too embarrassed to give the recipe.

Bubby's Chocolate Cake

1½ cups **sugar**

½ cup **cocoa**

2¼ cups **flour**

8 oz. **margarine**

1¼ tsp. **baking powder**

¾ tsp. **baking soda**

1½ cups **warm water**

1 tsp. **vanilla**

3 **eggs**

Beat together all ingredients except eggs, until batter is very smooth and shiny. The batter should look like chocolate mousse. Add eggs and beat again. Pour into a 9" x 13" pan or two 9" rounds. Bake at 350° for 30 – 35 minutes. Cool. Ice with Chocolate Fudge Icing.

This is the cake that saves the day. I am the cook that always things she doesn't have enough food. So, very often an hour before Shabbos you will find me baking another dessert, and this is it. I can get it in and out of the oven in 45 minutes.

Chocolate Cake Supreme

3 cups **flour**

1/2 tsp. **salt**

2 tsp. **baking powder**

13/4 cups **sugar**

1/2 cup **cocoa**

4 oz. **margarine**

1/2 cup **water**

1 tsp. **almond extract**

4 **eggs,** separated

Put all ingredients except egg whites in mixer and mix. In a separate bowl beat egg whites until stiff peaks form. Fold egg whites into cake batter and bake at 325° for 1 hour.

Chocolate Sinful Cake

12 oz. **bittersweet chocolate**

1 tsp. **instant coffee**

10 oz. **butter or margarine**, room temperature

11/4 cups **sugar**

10 **eggs**, separated

1 oz. **chocolate shavings**

Melt chocolate with coffee. Cream butter or margarine and sugar in a large bowl. Add cooled chocolate and blend well. Add egg yolks one at a time and beat on a low speed for 15 minutes.

Beat egg whites until stiff peaks form and fold them into the batter. Pour 3/4 of batter into a spring form and bake at 350° for 50 minutes. Let cake cool — it will sink in the middle. Spread remaining batter on top of cake. Cover and chill in refrigerator overnight. Garnish with chocolate shavings.

To be served on special occasions only, followed by three days of strict dieting.

Chocolate Velvet Cake

4 oz. **sweet or semisweet chocolate**, broken into pieces

6 Tbsp. **butter or margarine**

3 Tbsp. **flour**

3 **eggs**, separated

4 Tbsp. **sugar**

Melt chocolate and butter in saucepan over very low heat, stirring constantly until smooth. Remove from heat. Stir in flour. Blend in egg yolks, one at a time. Beat egg whites until foamy and gradually beat in sugar until soft peaks form. Gently fold chocolate mixture into egg whites, blending thoroughly. Pour into greased and floured 8" layer pan. Bake at 350° for approx. 20 minutes. Cool in pan 10 minutes. (Cake will settle.) Finish cooling upside down on cake rack. Spread top and sides with Glaze.

Glaze

4 oz. **chocolate**, broken into pieces

3 Tbsp. **water**

½ cup **sugar**

3 Tbsp. **butter or margarine**

Melt chocolate with water and sugar over low heat, stirring constantly. Remove from heat and stir in butter or margarine. Cool to thicken, if necessary. If left in the fridge too long and it hardens, heat up only momentarily to get stirring started, and it will return to proper consistency for glazing.

Easy Chocolate Mocha Cake

2 cups **flour**

2 cups **sugar**

1 cup **cocoa**

2 tsp. **baking soda**

2 **eggs**

2 cups **boiling coffee**

1 cup **mayonnaise**

Mix together first 4 ingredients, then add remaining ingredients. Place in a 9" x 13" pan or two 8" layer pans. Bake at 350° for ½ hour.

Cover with Chocolate Fudge Icing or Chocolate Mousse Icing (see Icings).

Broiled Coconut Icing

A perfect icing for any White Cake — especially Hot Milk Sponge Cake.

1 cup **coconut**

4 oz. **margarine**

1 cup **brown sugar**

2 – 3 Tbsp. **milk or parve cream**

Mix all ingredients in a saucepan and heat until sugar and margarine are melted and blended. Spread over warm cake. Return pan to oven, placing it under broiler for 10 minutes only, watching to see that it does not burn. It will bubble and caramelize.

Fudge Icing

2 oz. **margarine**

1/4 cup **water**

1/4 cup **cocoa**

1 cup **sugar**

Mix all ingredients in a saucepan and boil for one minute *only*, stirring constantly. Beat with an electric beater, being careful not to overbeat — just until it's thick enough to spread. As the icing cools, it hardens into a shiny glaze.

Cream Cheese Frosting

8 oz. **cream cheese**

6 Tbsp. **butter or margarine**

3 cups **powdered sugar**

1 tsp. **vanilla**

juice of ½ **lemon**

Cream together cream cheese and butter or margarine, and slowly sift powdered sugar into mixture. Mixture should be free of lumps. Add vanilla and lemon juice. Spread on cooled cake. This a delightful frosting for carrot cakes, and zucchini and banana breads.

Chocolate Mousse Icing

For a wonderful chocolate icing, see the Mousse Icing and Filling in the Pies chapter of this book. It may also be used for a filling between layers of cake.

Special Occasion Cake Icing

6 oz. **margarine**

1 lb. **powdered sugar**, sifted

2 tsp. **vanilla or mint flavoring**

2 Tbsp. **water or orange juice**

food coloring (optional)

Cream margarine and add sugar slowly. Add flavoring, water, and food coloring, if wanted. Orange juice may be used instead of flavorings. Makes 2 cups of icing.

COOKIES, SQUARES, and BARS

Applesauce Squares

2½ cups **self-rising flour**

1 cup **sugar**

1 tsp. **vanilla**

1 cup **margarine**

Filling

1 can **applesauce**

½ tsp. **lemon juice**

1 tsp. **cinnamon**

3 Tbsp. **sugar**

Crumb together first 4 ingredients and pat most of the mixture on the bottom of a 9" x 13" or a 10" square pan. Mix filling ingredients and pour onto this crust. Cover with remaining crumbs. Sprinkle extra cinnamon on top. Bake at 350° for 30 - 40 minutes.

Brown Sugar Thins

1 1b. **brown sugar**

1 lb. **butter or margarine**, softened

½ tsp. **vanilla**

4½ cups **flour**

Cream sugar, butter, and vanilla until fluffy. Work in flour until a soft dough forms. Pinch off small lumps of dough, then flatten and press very thin with flat bottom of a glass that has been greased and dipped in sugar.

Bake at 300° for 15 minutes, more or less, until cookies look slightly browner than the raw dough.

Brownies

1 cup **cocoa**

8 oz. **margarine**

2 cups **sugar**

4 **eggs**

1 cup **flour**

1 tsp. **vanilla**

½ tsp. **salt**

nuts and **chocolate chips** (optional)

Cream sugar and eggs. Add margarine and cocoa. Mix in flour, salt, and vanilla. Fold in nuts and/or chocolate chips.

Bake at 350° for 15 – 20 minutes. Cut while warm.

I try to underbake all brownies because I like them to be chewy.

Coffee Blond Brownies

1 lb. **brown sugar**

6 oz. **butter or margarine**

2 Tbsp. **instant coffee powder**

1 Tbsp. **hot water**

2 tsp. **vanilla**

2 **eggs**

2 cups **flour**

2 tsp. **baking powder**

½ tsp. **salt**

1 cup **pecans**

1 cup **chocolate chips**

Heat sugar and butter until melted. Dissolve coffee in water, and add to butter and sugar. Let cool. Mix next 4 ingredients together and stir into cooled mixture. Add nuts and chocolate chips.

Bake at 350° for 25 – 30 minutes.

Killer Brownies — Super Special

5 oz. **butter or margarine**

4 oz. **bittersweet chocolate**

1 cup **sugar**

1 cup **brown sugar**

3 **eggs**

1 tsp. **vanilla**

1 cup **flour**

1½ cups chopped **walnuts**

6 oz. **chocolate chips**

Melt butter and bittersweet chocolate together. Mix in sugars slowly. Beat in each egg individually. Add vanilla, flour, and half the walnuts. Pour into a greased 9" x 13" pan. If you like a thicker brownie, use a square pan. Mix chips and remaining walnuts together and sprinkle over mixture in pan, pressing them in. Bake at 350° for 18 – 20 minutes.

FLASH! This recipe is all mixed in one pot — by hand.

Mimi Baron discovered this recipe and made it for the Yeshiva boys so much that she decided to make new cookies for them instead. Still there is always someone to ask, "Mimi, where are the Killer Brownies?"

Butter Cookies #1

8 oz. **butter**

¾ cup **sugar**

3 **egg yolks**

2½ cups **flour**

1 tsp. **lemon juice**

grated **rind** of **1 lemon**

Mix all ingredients together and shape dough into a cylinder roll. Wrap well and chill in refrigerator for ½ hour. Dough should be slightly hard. Slice into cookie size — ⅛" thick — and place on a cookie sheet. Brush each cookie with extra egg yolk that has been beaten with 1 Tbsp. of water. Bake at 350° for 10 minutes.

HINT: It is a good idea to keep a few cookie rolls in the freezer to be used when unexpected company comes. However, I am never quite that organized.

Butter Cookies #2

1 **egg**

8 oz. **butter**

½ cup **sugar**

2½ cups **flour**

nuts (optional)

Shape into a 2" cylinder roll and chill for approx. 15 minutes. Slice into cookies and brush with egg yolk that has been beaten with 1 Tbsp. water. Bake at 375° for 10 – 12 minutes.

Chocolate Chip Cookies

2½ cups **flour**

1 tsp. **baking soda**

1 tsp. **salt**

8 oz. **margarine**

¾ cup **sugar**

¾ cup **brown sugar**

1 tsp. **vanilla**

2 **eggs**

2 cups **chocolate chips**

1 cup **nuts** (optional)

Sift flour, baking soda, and salt together and set aside. Combine margarine, sugars, vanilla, and eggs. Add flour mixture and stir well. Mix in chocolate chips and nuts.

Drop by teaspoonfuls on to an ungreased cookie sheet. Bake at 375° for 8 – 10 minutes.

Chocolate Chip Peanut Butter Squares

4 oz. **margarine or butter**

½ cup **peanut butter**

½ cup **sugar**

½ cup **brown sugar**

1 **egg**

2 Tbsp. **water**

1¼ cups **flour**

¾ tsp. **baking soda**

½ tsp. **baking powder**

¼ tsp. **salt**

1 cup **chocolate chips**

Cream all ingredients together using only ½ cup chocolate chips. Spread onto a cookie sheet or into a loaf pan.

Bake at 375° (a little higher than a medium oven) for 20 minutes. Remove and sprinkle ½ cup more of chocolate chips on top. Bake for another 5 minutes. Spread melted chips with a knife or spatula to form an icing.

Can be cut into squares while warm, or freeze and cut as you need them. They freeze very well, and I cut very small squares because these cookies are so rich and delicious.

Date Cookies

1 **egg**

4 oz. **margarine**, melted

1 cup **brown sugar**

1 cup **walnuts**

1 cup chopped **dates**

1 cup **self-rising flour**

Beat egg and mix in remaining ingredients. Bake in greased 9" square pan or double recipe for a 9" x 13" pan. Bake at 350° for 20 – 30 minutes. Cut into squares while still warm.

Sesame Squares

1 lb. **rolled oats** (oatmeal)

4 oz. **sesame seeds**

4 oz. **coconut**

2 oz. **wheatgerm**

2 oz. **nuts**

pinch of **salt**

1½ cups **oil**

5 – 6 **eggs**

1 cup **honey**

1 tsp. **vanilla**

Mix all ingredients and place onto a cookie sheet. Bake at 350° for 30 minutes. Cut while warm. When this cookie cools, it is a crisp, delightful, and healthy snack.

Coconut Almond Squares

2 **eggs**

1 cup **sugar**

1 cup **flour**

1 tsp. **baking powder**

½ tsp. **salt**

½ cup **milk**

1 Tbsp. melted **butter**

Mix all ingredients and pour into a 9" square pan. Bake at 350° for 30 minutes.

Topping

3 Tbsp. **butter**

5 Tbsp. **cream**

½ cup **brown sugar**

½ cup **coconut**

½ cup **chopped almonds**

Mix and spread over cake. Broil until bubbly and slightly brown. Do not let it burn!!!

Coconut Squares

Dough

8 oz. melted **margarine**

1 cup **brown sugar**

2 cups **flour**

Mix everything together. Press into pan and bake at 350°
for 15 minutes.

Topping

2 **eggs**

1 cup **brown sugar**

1 tsp. **vanilla**

2 Tbsp. **flour**

1/2 tsp. **baking powder**

1/4 tsp. **salt**

1 cup **coconut**

nuts (optional)

Mix everything together and spread on top of baked
cookie dough. Bake again for another 15 – 20 minutes.
    Cut into squares while warm.

Cream Cheese and Jelly Cookies

2 cups **Bisquick**

3/4 cup **heavy or light cream**

1/2 lb. **cream cheese**

1/2 cup **sugar**

cinnamon, nuts, sugar, coconut, jelly

Combine Bisquick and cream, and roll into a thick rectangle. Spread with mixture of cream cheese and sugar.
Sprinkle with cinnamon mixture. Roll up and cut into
small rounds. Bake on greased cookie sheet at 450° for
5 minutes only. Turn off heat and let cookies stay in the
oven for another 20 minutes.

*If Bisquick is not available, you can use my Scone dough
recipe (see Breads and Biscuits) instead of Bisquick and
cream mixture.*

Crunchies

12 oz. **butter or margarine**, melted

1 Tbsp. **honey**

½ tsp. **baking powder**

1 cup **oatmeal**

1 cup **coconut**

1 cup **sugar**

1½ cups **flour**

Mix first 3 ingredients, then add the rest.

Press into cookie tin and bake at 300° for 25 – 30 minutes. Cut into squares while hot, and remove from pan.

VARIATION
Chopped pecans can be added, or raisins. Whole wheat flour may also be used.

I discovered a wonderful secret about these cookies — they can be mixed in the pan — no bowls to wash. This is definitely my kind of recipe.

Doughnuts (Sufganiyot)

2 oz. **yeast**

1 cup **warm water**

½ cup **sugar**

1 tsp. **vanilla**

½ cup **margarine**, melted

3 **eggs**

5 – 5½ cups **flour**

jelly for filling

powdered sugar

Mix all ingredients into a soft dough. Let rise for 2 hours. Punch down and roll out. Cut into 3" rounds. Fill half the rounds with jelly, and wet the edges. Top with another circle and seal well. Let rise at least 20 minutes and fry in very hot oil. Lift out with a slotted spoon and drain. Dust with powdered sugar.

Ginger Snaps

3 oz. **margarine**, softened

1 cup **brown sugar**

¼ cup **molasses**

1 **egg**

2¼ cups **flour**

2 tsp. **baking soda**

1 tsp. **cinnamon**

1 tsp. **ginger**

Cream margarine, sugar, and molasses. Add egg, then add rest of ingredients.

Roll into balls and place on cookie sheet, leaving enough space in between for the cookie to spread out. Bake at 350° for 15 – 20 minutes.

Hamantashen

Cookie dough

1 cup **sugar**

3 – 4 cups **flour**

1½ tsp. **baking powder**

½ tsp. **salt**

8 oz. **butter or margarine**

2 **eggs**, beaten

½ cup **orange juice**

Mix dry ingredients together and cut in shortening until it is in small pieces. Add eggs and orange juice. Mix together into a soft ball. Roll out on a floured surface. Cut out rounds with a glass.

Filling

1 16 oz. jar **prune jam (lekvar)**

1 tsp. **lemon juice**

Mix jam with lemon juice. Put one teaspoon filling in center of each round. Pick up edges toward center to form a triangle and pinch dough together with floured fingers. Baste top with egg yolk diluted with a little bit of water.

Bake at 350° for approx. 30 minutes or until lightly browned.

February 25, 1991

If you check you calendar, you will note that in just four days, Purim will be here. There is a war, a frightening and horrible war. Each night we are plagued with missile attacks. Israel is strong — united and able to withstand all that is thrown at us. For the moment we are silent. Our strength comes from our ancestors who at this very time 2,500 years ago were able to turn the world around.

I have just made a batch of fifty-one Hamantashen to celebrate Purim on Friday. I hope that they last — but just to be sure, I will make 2 more batches before the week is out. One third of this batch has already disappeared thanks to my faithful tasters: the Yeshiva boys and Natie.

from Bubby Irma's Diary

Healthy Cookies

3 oz. **butter or margarine**

⅓ cup packed **brown sugar**

¼ cup **honey**

1 **egg**

1 tsp. **vanilla**

1½ cups **rolled oats** (oatmeal)

½ cup **whole wheat flour**

½ tsp. **salt**

½ tsp. **cinnamon**

2 cups **raisins**

½ cup **sesame seeds**

½ cup **coconut**

Cream together butter, sugar, and honey until light and creamy. Beat in egg and vanilla. Stir together the next 7 ingredients.

Drop by rounded teaspoonfuls onto greased baking sheets. Bake at 350° for approx. 15 minutes or until cookies are golden brown.

Makes 2½ dozen cookies.

Heavenly Bits

8 oz. **margarine or butter**

4 Tbsp. **powdered sugar**

1 tsp. **water**

2 tsp. **vanilla**

2 cups **flour**

1 cup **nuts** — pecans are preferred

Cream margarine and sugar well. Mix in remaining ingredients.Shape into finger-length rolls or form quarter-size balls and bake at 350° for 20 minutes.

While cookies are still warm, roll them in additional powdered sugar.

Jam Finger Cookies

4 oz. **margarine**

¼ cup **sugar**

1 **egg yolk**

1 cup **flour**

1 **egg white**, unbeaten

¾ cup **chopped nuts**

jam

Mix first 4 ingredients. Make marble-sized balls. Dip into unbeaten egg white, then into chopped nuts. Flatten with palm or knife on cookie sheet. Bake for 5 minutes. Remove from oven and press finger in center of each cookie — careful not to burn your finger. Place tray back in oven and bake an additional 15 minutes.

Using a small teaspoon, place jam in middle while cookies are warm.

Linzertorte Squares

8 oz. **margarine**

1 cup **sugar**

1 tsp. **vanilla**

2 **eggs**

3 – 3½ cups **flour**

1 cup **chopped nuts**

jam or jelly

Cream first 3 ingredients and add eggs, flour, and nuts. Spread onto cookie sheet, saving ¼ of dough for strips. Spread dough with jam or jelly. Press remaining dough into strips ½" wide and place them diagonally on the dough in a lattice pattern.

Bake at 350° for 20 minutes. Watch to see that edges don't burn. If edges get dark, cut them off and put remainder back in oven if necessary.

Mandelbroit

3 **eggs**

1 cup **sugar**

3 cups **flour**

2 tsp. **baking powder**

3/4 cup **oil**

1 tsp. **vanilla**

1 cup **almonds**

½ cup **raisins**

Mix everything together. Shape into 4 loaves in a cookie pan and bake at 350° for 30 minutes. Cut into 1" slices and return to cookie pan. Bake for another 20 – 30 minutes, turning once. Mix sugar and cinnamon and sprinkle on top (optional).

HINT: *Chocolate chips added to this recipe make it richer and even tastier, and it satisfies the choco-holics in the crowd.*

Peanut Butter Kisses

1 cup **smooth peanut butter**

¾ cup firmly packed **light brown sugar**

1 **egg**

1 tsp. **vanilla**

¼ cup **semisweet chocolate chips**

Combine peanut butter, brown sugar, egg, and vanilla in a large bowl. Stir until smooth. Roll dough into small balls. Place on ungreased cookie sheet about 1" apart and flatten a bit. Place one chocolate chip into the center of each cookie.

Bake in a preheated 300° oven for 20 minutes or until light brown. Store in a tight container.

Nanaimo Bars

No baking

Layer #1

4 oz. **butter or margarine**

¼ cup **sugar**

1 **egg**

1 tsp. **vanilla**

1 Tbsp. **cocoa**

Layer #2

2 cups **cookie crumbs**

1 cup **coconut**

½ cup **chopped nuts**

Layer #3

3 Tbsp. **milk**

2 cups **icing sugar**

2 Tbsp. **instant vanilla pudding**

2 oz. **butter or margarine**

Layer #4

4 oz. **semisweet chocolate**

1 Tbsp. **butter**

Layer #1: Mix ingredients together and heat in a double boiler. Stir until mixture thickens. Place mixture in a 9" x 9" square pan.

Layer #2: Mix and spread over layer #1. Refrigerate for 15 minutes.

Layer #3: Melt milk, sugar, and custard over hot water, but *do not* allow water to boil. Very slowly and gently stir in margarine or butter until it has just blended. Spread over Layer #2.

Layer #4: Melt together and spread over layer #3.
     Refrigerate and cut into bars when ready to serve.

Seven-Layered Cookies

4 oz. **margarine or butter**, melted

1 cup **cookie crumbs**

1 cup **coconut**

8 oz. **chocolate chips**

1 cup **pecans**

1 pkg. **butterscotch chips** (optional)

1 cup **sweetened condensed milk**

In a 9" x 13" pan (or on a cookie sheet) add all ingredients in separate layers. Do not stir. Dribble condensed milk over everything and let set for 15 minutes.
     Bake at 350° for 30 minutes. Flatten slightly with spatula and cool. Cut into squares.

Rugelach

Dough

4 cups **flour**

½ cup **sugar**

1 lb. **butter or margarine**

3 **eggs**

2 oz. **yeast**

1 cup **warm water**

Put flour into a bowl, make a well in the center and add sugar, melted margarine, eggs, and yeast dissolved in warm water. Mix well by hand or use dough hook of electric beater. Dough will be sticky and loose. Store in refrigerator for 5 – 6 hours or overnight.

Filling

2 cups **sugar**

cinnamon

raisins

chopped **pecans**

coconut

Divide dough into eight balls. Blend sugar and cinnamon together. Place a generous handful of sugar and cinnamon on the board, and knead a ball into it, letting dough absorb sugar and cinnamon. Roll out ball into 8" circle and sprinkle generously with nuts and coconut. Cut circle into 16 pieces, as if you are cutting pie slices. On each slice place 1 or 2 raisins and roll each slice toward the middle to form rugelach.

Bake at 350° for 20 minutes. Makes 128 rugelach.

Pinwheel Cookies

1 lb. **margarine**

1⅓ cups **sugar**

2 tsp. **vanilla**

4 cups **flour**

6 Tbsp. **cocoa**

Mix first four ingredients together. Divide dough in half and add cocoa to one half of dough. Roll out doughs — 1 white roll and 1 chocolate roll — then roll the two together like a jelly roll, and cut into cookie rounds.

Place cookies on a cookie sheet and bake at 400° for 7 – 10 minutes.

Sour Cream Fruit Squares

Base

8 oz. **margarine**

½ cup **sugar**

2 **eggs**

2½ cups **self-rising flour**

1 pkg. **vanilla sugar**

Mix everything together and pat into cookie tin. Bake at 350° for 25 minutes.

Topping

1 16 oz. can **apricots, pineapple, or peaches,** drained

8 oz. **margarine**

¾ cup **sugar**

2 **eggs**

2 pkgs. **vanilla sugar**

1 pint (2 cups) **sour cream**

Place fruit onto baked crust. Spoon sour cream mixture over fruit. Bake 10 minutes more. Cut into squares while warm.

DESSERTS

Brandied Oranges

4 **oranges**, sliced thin with rind

¾ cup **sugar**

¾ cup **water**

¼ cup **orange juice**

1 tsp. **lemon juice**

1 Tbsp. **brandy**

Marinate oranges in sauce ingredients for ½ hour before serving.

Cream Cheese and Pineapple Mold

2 pkgs. **lemon jello**

1¼ cups **hot water**

1 lb. **cream cheese or cottage cheese**

1 large can **crushed pineapple** plus 1 cup **juice** from can

Mix jello and water. Cool. Stir in cheese and pineapple with juice. Put into mold and chill.

Parve Ice Cream #1

6 **eggs**

½ cup **sugar**

½ cup **oil**

½ pkg. **instant vanilla pudding**

Beat in electric mixer for 10 minutes and freeze.

Parve Ice Cream #2

1 cup **strawberries**

6 **eggs**

1¼ cups **sugar**

1 cup **oil**

¼ cup **orange juice**

Blend strawberries in blender. Mix all ingredients together, cook until hot, then blend again, and put into freezer.

Peanut Butter Cups

1 cup **smooth peanut butter**

1 lb. **powdered sugar** (approx. 2 scant cups)

1¼ lbs. **bittersweet chocolate**

4 oz. **butter or margarine**

Mix peanut butter and powdered sugar together and put teaspoons of mixture in small cupcake papers (preferably in small-size cupcake tins) and press firmly into place. Melt chocolate with butter. Pour melted mixture over peanut butter in cups and freeze for 10 – 15 minutes.

Yields 75 peanut butter cups.

Spiced Pears

6 whole **pears**, peeled

½ cup **water**

½ cup **white wine**

⅔ cup **honey**

3 Tbsp. **lemon juice**

1 tsp. **lemon rind**

2 tsp. **cinnamon**

1 tsp. **nutmeg**

1 tsp. **cloves**

Place all ingredients into a saucepan and allow to simmer for 20 minutes. Serve hot or cold with cream or ice cream.

Strawberry and Pineapple Jello

2 pkgs. **jello, strawberry or cherry**

1½ cups **boiling water**

3 cups sliced **strawberries**

1 16 oz. can **crushed pineapple**, drained well

1 cup **juice from pineapple can**

1 cup or more **sour cream**

Dissolve jello in boiling water. Add strawberries and pineapple plus juice from pineapple.

Spoon half the mixture into a square dish and refrigerate until set. Frost with a layer of sour cream and refrigerate for another ½ hour. Spoon on remainder of mixture and refrigerate until used. Comes out well in a greased jello mold.

Yogurt Pudding

1 cup **heavy cream**

2 cups **yogurt**

2 **apples**

1 tsp. **sugar**

nuts

Whip cream and fold into yogurt. Grate apples and add to cream mixture. Fold in chopped nuts, saving some for garnishing. Spoon into serving dishes and chill.

The House of Charles: Personal Tributes

My first encounter with the House of Charles took place 6½ years ago. We were on a family trip to visit my two brothers who were studying in Jerusalem. Little did I know that my first-ever Shabbos experience would herald my entrance as an honorary member of the Charles Family.

My return to study the following summer firmly established Irma and Natie's place as my "home away from home." Along with the house came Irma's cooking. I have long since become addicted to Irma's Chocolate Mousse Cake, not to mention her Mocha Chicken, Potato Knishes with Mushroom Sauce, Babka — the list is endless.

In those early years, I was living in a dormitory, so it was not unusual for Irma and Natie to let me move into the house when they went away. One Shabbos, Irma insisted that I use one of the myriad dishes stuffed into her freezer (which I have yet to see even partially empty in six years). She pointed out a container and said, "That's Chicken and Wine — just make some rice to go with it." I remember being amazed how Irma remembered what was in her freezer without labeling anything.

Erev Shabbos rolled around, and I pulled out the dish and set it defrosting on the stove. Lo and behold! Irma's Chicken and Wine was really Chicken Soup in disguise. Not to worry — it was delicious.

I am married now and my two children are honorary Charles grandchildren. Challah made according to Irma's recipe is always at my Shabbos table.

Rebecca Spiro Shore

Bubby Irma,

I am going to start this off by saying "Bubby" is not really appropriate. "Ema" is a more suitable title, for Irma is far too young, too beautiful, and way too "hep" to be labelled "Bubby!"

Every child dreams of having a mother who is warm and sensitive to his or her needs — a mother who does not try to make her child do what she was not capable of accomplishing herself. We hope for somebody who will always be there, through good times and bad, ready with a few special words so we will know that everything is going to be okay. Irma is not only a mother, but also a best friend. Anyone who know Irma Charles feels this when in her presence. Irma Charles is everything I hope to be when, *be'ezrat Hashem*, I become a mother myself.

Being in Irma's kitchen with her while she cooks and prepares for Shabbos is the most beautiful gift that a yeshiva student can experience. Cooking with Irma is like creating the most wonderful piece of art one can imagine. It's always so interesting to watch her face as she tastes the batter to detect that special something that is needed to make it perfect. I have never met anybody who cooks with as much love as Irma does.

One can never experience the Shechinah of Hashem until he has come to Eretz Yisrael. It is the Promised Land, and I now understand why! But, as beautiful as it is to be in Eretz Yisrael, being here without family can sometimes be extremely painful. The Charleses have managed to make their home a place where anyone can go when he needs to feel loved.

I only pray that I am able to accomplish the same.

I love you, Irma and Natie.

Love always,
Heather

The "House of Charles" is an institution in the Jewish Quarter! My family is blessed with the good fortune of having a relationship with the entire Charles family. My parents in Toronto and my siblings here and abroad have all experienced the warmth and selfless giving of Irma and Natie.

Our family has had many *simchahs* here in the past few years, and all of them have been closely intertwined with the House of Charles. We have had a bar mitzvah, two engagement announcements, and a sheva brachos in this very special home, as well as countless Shabbos and Holiday meals (and lots of everyday meals too).

The highlight for me was the sheva brachos that took place the night after our wedding. There were thirty people, mostly family members, who came in from near and far for the wedding. Most were leaving the next day. There were so many tears shed and warm hugs shared, that all the families (Pamensky, Charles, and Fox) instantly became one.

Who could ask for a better start for our new life together? This is only one of the countless special moments in the Charleses' home for me and my whole family.

Aryeh and Jaymie (Charles) Pamensky

Scuds and Scones

When Iraq's Sadaam Hussein started threatening to send missiles to Israel during the fall of 1990, there was no question where I would go if his threats were to become reality. I would move into the House of Charles, because, as Natie says, "You're one of us."

On January 15th, 1991, the night the Allies were to begin bombing Baghdad, I moved into the Charleses' house along with two other friends. Ostensibly, we would be there to help Irma and Natie. In reality, we needed them as much as they needed us.

It was a night of anticipation. Would Bush really begin the war? Most importantly, we asked ourselves the key question: What is the Al-Mighty trying to tell us? After all the special classes on doing *teshuvah* and good deeds, after all the fasting and prayers, we were suddenly living in a new spiritual reality where every moment counted.

At about 1:50 A.M. one of the guests shouted out, "The war's started! The war's started!"

Irma and Natie woke up and we all crowded around the radio, wondering when the scuds would begin flying towards us.

We started calling family and friends to wake them up and make sure they were ready. Many people, including my brother, went to work putting their finishing touches on their sealed rooms. Irma and I were itchy to do something too.

What is more appropriate for Irma to do at a time like this than to bake? At 3:30 in the morning, we went to work baking he famous scones. I've never been a big scone fan, but that night it tasted like manna. The scones came out big and heavy. For the heartiest appetites, one is more than plenty. Let me tell you, Natie alone ate five. We guests ate at least three each.

This is just a small taste of the love and laughter that is found in the House of Charles. Irma, I love you, Natie, and your entire family. I could write my own book about you and it would be a best seller too! For you readers, all I can say is enjoy this book and be sure to stop by and meet these wonderful people the next time you are in the Old City!

Mimi Baron

INDEX